CRACL

GW01417830

Translation Practices Exp

Translation Practices Explained is a series of coursebooks designed to help self-learners and teachers of translation. Each volume focuses on a specific aspect of professional translation practice, in many cases corresponding to actual courses available in translator-training institutions. Special volumes are devoted to well consolidated professional areas, such as legal translation or European Union texts; to areas where labour-market demands are currently undergoing considerable growth, such as screen translation in its different forms; and to specific aspects of professional practices on which little teaching and learning material is available, the case of editing and revising, or electronic tools. The authors are practising translators or translator trainers in the fields concerned. Although specialists, they explain their professional insights in a manner accessible to the wider learning public.

These books start from the recognition that professional translation practices require something more than elaborate abstraction or fixed methodologies. They are located close to work on authentic texts, and encourage learners to proceed inductively, solving problems as they arise from examples and case studies.

Each volume includes activities and exercises designed to help self-learners consolidate their knowledge; teachers may also find these useful for direct application in class, or alternatively as the basis for the design and preparation of their own material. Updated reading lists and website addresses will also help individual learners gain further insight into the realities of professional practice.

Dorothy Kelly
Series Editor

A Handbook for Translator Trainers
A Guide to Reflective Practice

Dorothy Kelly

St. Jerome Publishing
Manchester, UK & Northampton MA

Published by
  St. Jerome Publishing (Manchester, UK & Northampton, USA)
  2 Maple Road West, Brooklands
  Manchester, M23 9HH, United Kingdom
  Tel +44 161 973 9856
  Fax +44 161 905 3498
  stjerome@compuserve.com
  http://www.stjerome.co.uk

ISBN 978-1-900650-81-6 (pbk)
ISSN 1470-966X (*Translation Practices Explained*)

© Dorothy Kelly 2005; reprinted 2012

All rights reserved, including those of translation into foreign languages. No part of this publication may be reproduced, stored in a retrieval system or transmitted in any form or by any means, electronic, mechanical, photocopying, recording or otherwise without either the prior written permission of the Publisher or a licence permitting restricted copying issued by the Copyright Licensing Agency (CLA), 90 Tottenham Court Road, London, W1P 9HE. In North America, registered users may contact the Copyright Clearance Center (CCC): 222 Rosewood Drive, Danvers MA 01923, USA.

Typeset by
Delta Typesetters, Cairo, Egypt
Email: hilali1945@yahoo.co.uk

British Library Cataloguing in Publication Data
A catalogue record of this book is available from the British Library

Library of Congress Cataloging-in-Publication Data
Kelly, Dorothy Anne. A handbook for translator trainers : a guide to reflective practice / Dorothy Kelly.
  p. cm. -- (Translation practices explained)
  Includes bibliographical references and index.
  ISBN 1-900650-81-9 (pbk. : alk. paper)
  1. Translators--Training of. I. Title. II. Series.
  P306.5K459 2005
  418'.02'0711--dc22

                        2005017808

Printed and bound in Great Britain by 4edge Ltd, Hockley, Essex.

Contents

List of Figures

List of Abbreviations

ALE	Applied Languages Europe triple degree programme
ATA	American Translators Association
AVANTI	Avances en Traducción e Interpretación Research Group, Universidad de Granada, Spain
BDÜ	Bundesverband der Dolmetscher und der Übersetzer
CILT	National Centre for Languages
CIUTI	Conférence Internationale Permanente d'Instituts Universitaires de Traducteurs e d'Interprètes/ International Permanent Conference of University Institutes of Translators and Interpreters
EST	European Society for Translation Studies
EU	European Union
FIT	Fédération Internationale de Traducteurs/International Federation of Translators
IATIS	International Association for Translation and Intercultural Studies
ITI	Institute for Translation and Interpreting
ITIA	Irish Translators' and Interpreters' Association
LNTO	Languages National Training Organization
NZSTI	New Zealand Society of Translators and Interpreters
PACTE	Proceso de Adquisición de la Competencia Traductora y Evaluación Research Group, Universitat Autònoma de Barcelona, Spain
SATI	South African Translators' Institute
SFT	Société Française des Traducteurs
SOLO	Structure of the Observed Learning Outcome
Temcu	Training Teachers for the Multicultural Classroom at University
TI	Translating and Interpreting
TRAP	Translation Process Research Group, Copenhagen Business School, Denmark
TS	Translation Studies

Acknowledgements

This book is reflects almost thirty years' experience in translator training programmes, first as a student at Heriot-Watt University in the UK and at the École de Traducteurs et d'Interprètes in Geneva, and later as a teacher at the Universidad de Granada in Spain, alongside short teaching missions at other universities and professional experience of different kinds as a translator and interpreter. It inevitably owes a great deal to many people who have shaped my approach to teaching in different ways over the years: my father as a teacher himself; my own teachers, especially those at Heriot-Watt; my colleagues in Granada and in many other universities in Spain and abroad with whom I have had the opportunity to work; and above all, my students, from whom I have learned much more than they from me over the years. Special mention should be made here of postgraduate students since 1998 and indeed short summer course participants since 1991, who have unwittingly piloted and validated earlier versions of much of the material used here. Amongst my colleagues, on this occasion particular thanks must go to Roberto Mayoral and to Catherine Way for their constant support, encouragement and always constructive criticism, and especially for their very helpful comments on the first draft of this book. I am very grateful to Elvira Cámara, who very generously took on some of my workload to give me enough time to complete the manuscript. Special thanks are also due to Anne Martin, for being there unfailingly all these years; to all the members of the AVANTI research group, for their time, for their dedication and their support; to other close colleagues in Granada; to colleagues on European projects I have had the pleasure to participate in (most specially, ALE and Temcu); to very dear colleagues at other universities in Spain and elsewhere, from all of whom I have learned much: they are too numerous to name, for which my sincere apologies. I am deeply grateful to Mona and Ken Baker at St Jerome for the trust they have placed in me. And finally to Rafa, Dani and Sara, to whom I owe much more than I can hope to give in return.

How to Use this Book

The main aim of this book is to provide a useful tool to those involved in translator training in the planning of their teaching. Translator trainers come from many different academic and professional backgrounds: this is a job where translators, language teachers and Translation Studies (TS) scholars come together, with a wide range of levels of experience in translating, in researching and in teaching. The book aspires to offer something to all of these groups, in that its primary intention is to offer substantial food for thought to trainers, in order to facilitate the complex task of curricular and syllabus design. I stress throughout the need for attention to be paid to the specific context in which training or teaching is taking place. It would not be coherent, from this perspective, to propose a set of one-size-fits-all solutions to the different issues and problems arising in translator training. The book does not, therefore, propose objectives, activities, tasks, projects, syllabuses, or full curricula for implementation on all translator training programmes. It aims, rather, to promote reflection and to help readers to reach conclusions which are appropriate to their own course, institution and regional or national setting. The approach taken has been to put forward the basic educational considerations for each step in the design process, to give examples and analyse them, and then to encourage readers to carry out their own analysis and design their own curriculum, syllabus, projects, tasks and activities, based on their own aims and intended outcomes.

The book centres on training, and for this reason presupposes knowledge of translation as a discipline and as a professional activity; those from outside the field of TS should not expect to find here subject matter expertise in translation itself, as there is already a huge wealth of literature available to cover very different needs in that area.

Although I believe strongly that the similarities between interpreting and translating as forms of social, cultural and linguistic mediation are much greater than the differences between them, this book centres only on translator training. The general curricular design approach taken up in the book is, of course, applicable to interpreter training, but I feel that, despite the similarities, the specificities of the interpreting professions and training for them merit separate treatment in a sister publication.

TS has often been described as an interdisciplinary or multidisciplinary field of study, and there is no doubt that as a complex social, cultural, textual, and cognitive activity, translation can only benefit from input from many different perspectives. Despite widespread consensus on this belief in our field, it is also the case that TS has also often adopted rather blinkered views, perhaps driven by the perceived need to consolidate itself as an independent discipline. Just as this has happened in other branches of our discipline, it is very much the case that the debate on training translators has only rarely transcended our self-imposed disciplinary borders to take into account wider issues of higher education and training. An attempt is made here to bring together considerations from TS itself, and from the field of Education, in particular from research carried out into Higher Education and Curricular Studies. I am deeply aware that there is still a tremendous amount of work to be done in this direction, but hope that some of the issues dealt with in these pages will serve to encourage more colleagues to delve into the fascinating worlds these disciplines offer us, and to take advantage of the enormous amount of work already carried out as a basis on which to build their own approaches to or research into translator training.

The book proceeds according to a systematic approach to curricular and syllabus design. It has thus been organized in chapters dealing with individual aspects of translator training from the most general to the most specific, and in the order in which most curricular decision-making processes are carried out (although there is clearly a great deal of interrelation and much of the process is recursive in nature). The text may therefore be read chronologically, from beginning to end, but it has also been planned so that chapters may be read as self-contained units. Trainers interested specifically, for example, in teaching resources may go straight to the corresponding chapter to find the issue dealt with in depth without any need to have read previous chapters. Each chapter begins with a brief summary of what it intends to achieve, contains practical activities for the reader, aimed mainly at encouraging reflection on current and future practice, and ends with a brief review and recommendations on further reading. In the further reading sections, an attempt has been made to identify short but useful texts for non-specialists when dealing with higher education issues not specific to the field of TS; TS references, on the other hand, are more numerous and often refer to more in-depth studies, many of which may already be familiar to the reader.

True to the overall approach, designed to promote reflection and to encourage readers to critically engage all the elements involved in curricular design (including the ideas put forward in the book itself), the activities constitute an important part of the book. If active participation promotes higher-level learning, then here too, I hope, carrying out the activities may lead to greater involvement, deeper reflection and more appropriate conclusions. The activities may be carried out alone or, better, in small groups; they could also form the basis for short staff development, or trainer training courses.

Systematic approaches to curricular design take as their starting point the institutional and social context in which training is to take place, and from there establish their objectives or intended outcomes with input from the professional sector for which students are to be trained, from society at large and from the academic disciplines involved; careful attention is paid to the resources available, and to the profile of the participants involved: students and teaching staff.

Teaching and learning activities are designed with a view to attaining the learning outcomes desired, are carefully sequenced and coordinated with each other and with assessment. Assessment includes not only evaluation of the degree of attainment of the learning outcomes established for the programme, but also the functioning of the programme itself, with a view to identifying areas for improvement. The final stage thus closes the circle, in that it consists of incorporating into programme content, organization and activities any innovation and improvement identified as necessary by the evaluation process. The process is represented in diagrammatic form in figure 1.

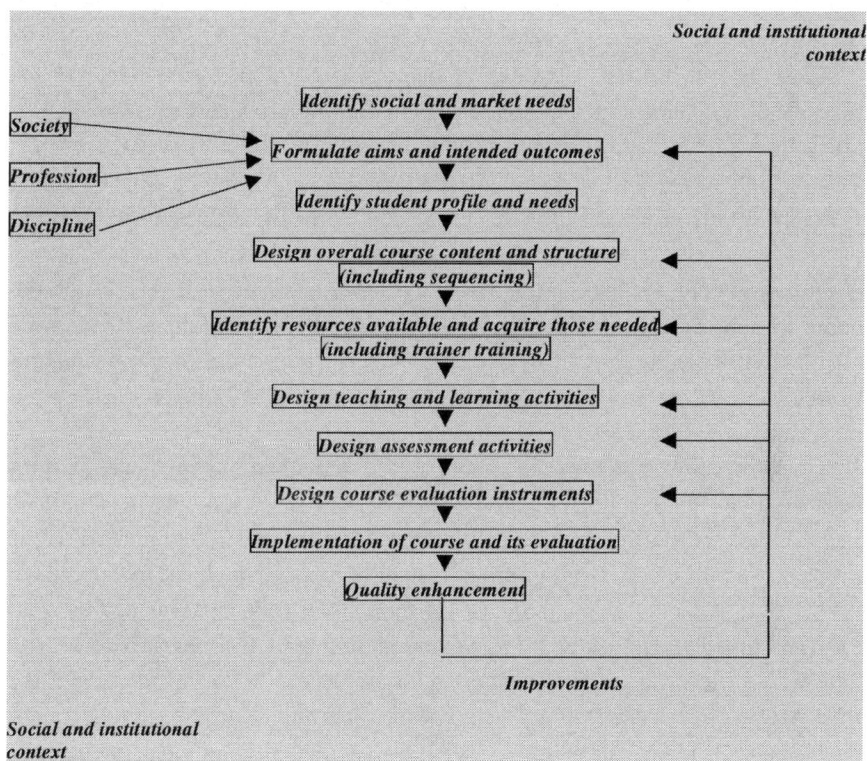

Figure 1. Curricular design process

A slightly simplified version of this figure will appear at the beginning of each chapter from Chapter 2 onwards. The idea is to situate our reflections at the appropriate point in the design process, highlighting the stage or stages discussed in each chapter.

The initial chapter of the book is intended to serve as an introduction to translator training, by briefly sketching its evolution and then offering an overview of major recent literature in translator training. There is a huge amount of literature available on this subject, making it impossible to review (or even read!) it all. For this reason, only some of the principal authors and their ideas are reviewed. Any selection of this kind necessarily implies omission; in this case an attempt has been made to choose authors who are particularly representative of different approaches to the learning and teaching process, rather than their TS tradition or approach. Reference will be made throughout the book at pertinent points to these and to many other authors who have made valuable contributions to the field of translator training. It is my view that on very few occasions can a single proposal meet all the very distinct requirements a training course presents, and that the contributions of all the authors mentioned have a great deal to offer our field, when used in a way appropriate to our own situations or contexts.

Chapter 2 marks the beginning of our actual curricular or syllabus design process, as it deals with the outcomes of the training process. From the systematic approach used in this book, it is essential to establish first and foremost what we intend to achieve. This chapter looks at how this can be done by taking into account the profession, the discipline and the institutional setting for training. Professional standards, theoretical work on translator competence and overall institutional contexts and "missions" all serve as sources to be taken into account when formulating aims and objectives or intended outcomes. Readers are encouraged to formulate aims and outcomes for their own local and institutional contexts, taking into account all possible environmental factors and constraints.

Chapter 3 moves on to the agents involved in the learning and teaching process: students and teachers. Teaching and learning are essentially personal and interpersonal activities, making the people involved absolutely central to the process. The importance of taking into account features such as students' prior knowledge, personal characteristics, learning styles, expectations and motivation, and the degree of group homogeneity is discussed. Similar factors are also analysed for teaching staff, an aspect often neglected in curricular design; the importance of coordination and team work on complex training programmes such as ours is also dealt with. Needs analysis which although to some extent a form of assessment is closely related to student profile, is also covered in this chapter.

The next step is that of defining content, discussed in Chapter 4. Once again, the variety of situations in which translators are trained and work professionally means that no one set of essential elements is proposed. Amongst the issues addressed, partly through case studies of existing or proposed courses are: academic versus vocational contexts; undergraduate versus postgraduate models; level of specialization. A series of examples of actual course structures are then presented, the first of which is analysed in depth. Finally, the major areas of translator competence are discussed briefly in relation to course content.

Curricular design should take into account existing resources and identify others needed for successful implementation of the programme planned. Chapter 5 offers an overview of potential resources, a term taken in the broadest possible sense, covering both traditional and less traditional resources normally at the disposal of translator trainers. The chapter moves from the basics of physical environment (how are our classrooms furnished and laid out?) through traditional resources (textbooks or the blackboard) to new technologies, analysing the advantages and disadvantages of each of these specifically for translator training. It then moves on to look at less traditional kinds of teaching and learning resources, such as mobility programmes and work placements.

Chapter 6 moves on to teaching and learning itself, to methods, techniques and activities. Here, the main issues covered are the design of different types of exercise and activity for specific outcomes, team or group work, in-class and out-of-the-classroom activities, and support and mentoring. Particular importance is given to the need for direct links (alignment) between teaching and learning activities on the one hand and learning outcomes as discussed in chapter two on the other, bearing in mind the participants (chapter 3) and resources available (chapter 5).

Clearly, not all activities are suitable for all levels of learning, so Chapter 7 deals with progression and sequencing. In TS long-standing debates relating to progression have been whether theory or practice should come first, or whether language skills should be acquired prior to translator training or simultaneous with it. These issues are addressed briefly before moving on to discuss the sequencing of types of activity, on the one hand, and the selection of texts for translation practice, on the other. A set of possible criteria for progression is suggested. Finally, we look at some ideas on how to involve trainees in the selection of materials and activities.

Chapter 8 deals with the complex issue of assessment and evaluation. Again this notion is understood in as wide a sense as possible. The chapter covers formative and summative assessment as part of teaching and learning; the importance of feedback; peer assessment; self assessment; traditional and innovative ways of assessing translator competence; individual versus group assessment. Finally, evaluation of teaching and programmes is also addressed briefly.

The last chapter of the book takes a look at the question of trainer training, at resources currently available for new trainers, or those in search of some form of continuing staff development. The design of trainer training is approached systematically, beginning with the establishment of intended outcomes, and moving through learner profiles to content, activities and assessment. The chapter also includes a conclusion to the reflections put forward throughout the book.

At the back of the book, readers will find a short glossary of the main terms relating to translator training used in the book. These are indicated at first usage from Chapter 1 by the use of bold face. Finally, a full list of references, including works cited and those recommended for further reading, is included.

I trust that all the different questions put forward and the discussions thereof will give rise to reflection, analysis and criticism. I will be very grateful for feedback from readers on any aspect covered, in particular on the usefulness of the activities for readers included in the book, and of course on errors, inaccuracies and omissions.

Dorothy Kelly
Granada, April 2005
dkelly@ugr.es

1. Setting the Scene

Summary and aims

This initial chapter has two main parts. Firstly, it takes a brief look at translator training in its historical, social, professional and academic settings, with the aim of contextualizing the issues dealt with throughout the book. The chapter will consider, among other aspects some historical antecedents and the appearance of the first institutional training courses; different types of training; academic and vocational courses available; the role of professional and academic associations and training; the role of industry in training. As there are regional and national differences in the way in which translator training has evolved, the aim of the chapter is in no way to offer information on all contexts, but rather pointers which will help readers to situate their own regional and national tradition, and to reflect on the implications of working in that particular context for training design and decisions. Secondly, the chapter offers an overview of major recent literature on translator training. To this end principal authors and their approaches are reviewed briefly. In carrying out such reviews, it has been customary to group authors according to their theoretical school, and it is certainly true that each author's translational approach influences training proposals in some way. For the purpose of this book on training for trainers, however, I have found that grouping authors from a methodological perspective is more appropriate. Hence rather than moving from contrastive approaches, through the *théorie du sens* to functionalism, cognitive approaches and so on, I have preferred to begin with the so-called traditional approach to training, through the first objective-based teaching proposals in our field, moving on to other **learner-centred** pedagogical approaches, or to highly professionalized situational approaches, as general headings under which loosely to classify leading authors and approaches. By the end of the chapter, readers should be familiar with major authors and their overall approaches. Further reading is strongly recommended.

Brief history

It is probably true to say that with few exceptions – such as the Colbert decree in France in 1669, which set up formal training for interpreters between French and Turkish, Arabic and Persian (Caminade and Pym, 1998) – institutional translator training is a phenomenon which begins in the mid twentieth century. Until then translators were essentially either language specialists or bilinguals, self-taught in translation, or with some form of apprenticeship or mentoring alongside more experienced colleagues. Indeed, a certain percentage of today's translators still enter the profession in this way, both in countries with institutional training courses and in countries where these do not (yet) exist. Self-taught and informally trained translators will probably continue to join the ranks of the profession, given the nature of the activity and the sectors in which it is carried out. However, they now account for a much smaller proportion of those employed or self-employed as professional translators as the institutionalization of training has proved to be a powerful and irreversible movement.

According to information offered by the institutions themselves, the oldest of the institutions devoted to generalist translator (and/or interpreter) training are the Moscow Linguistic University (ex-Maurice Thorez Institute, founded in 1930), the Ruprecht-Karls-Universität Heidelberg (1933), the Université de Genéve (1941) and the Universität Wien (1943), with a second group appearing after the Second World War in the Universität Innsbrück (1945), the Karl-Franzens-Universität Graz (1946), the Universität Johannes Gutenberg Mainz (at Germersheim, 1947), or the Universität des Saarlandes (at Saarbrücken, 1948). Two French institutions (École Supérieure d'Interprètes et de Traducteurs and Institut Supérieur d'Interprètes et de Traducteurs) followed in the fifties, the decade in which the CIUTI, or Conférence Internationale Permanente d'Instituts Universitaires de Traducteurs de d'Interprètes, an association of prestigious university training courses, was formed in order to:

> ...ensure the quality of professional translation and interpretation and thus meet the needs of the ever changing global professional environment for highly qualified translators and interpreters, [...] to contribute to the development of research in translation and interpretation and to the continued development of the training of professional translators and interpreters across the world. (www.ciuti.org)

The growing need for professional translators and interpreters both in bilingual contexts and due to the internationalization of the economy, later led to the founding or extension of courses in an increasing number of countries (Belgium, Canada, Italy, Netherlands, Australia, Denmark, UK, Spain...). Caminade and Pym (1998) calculate that the figure of approximately 250 courses worldwide was reached in the 1990s, and despite apparent saturation in some parts of the world, the figure certainly has not fallen since then, as countries such as Portugal, South Corea, or Poland set up their own programmes. The Intercultural Studies Group offers a list of existing translator training institutions at http://isg.urv.es/tti/tti.htm.

> When were the first translator training courses set up in your country/ context? How many are currently in operation? What differentiates your course from others in the same country?

Types of institutional training

Not all of these programmes take the same form. National contexts and traditions mean that some of them are full undergraduate courses (Germany, Belgium, Spain, Canada), while others are postgraduate (France, US, many but not all UK courses). Some are fully integrated into the university system and thus linked to departments which also conduct research; these tend to include a higher proportion of theoretical elements. Others are offered by institutions which do not belong entirely to the university system, granting vocational diplomas which do not lead on to postgraduate education, and tend not to include, or to include only a minimum of, theoretical content.

The aims of the programmes vary also from very generalist training, to training in specific areas of translation (literary translation, technical translation, legal translation, audiovisual or screen translation, conference interpreting, community interpreting). Length varies from short one year courses to long courses of up to five years.

> What are the general characteristics of your course: under- or postgraduate? Academic or vocational? Generalist or specialized? Long or short?

Professional associations and training

Of course, just as early translators were not trained at universties, not all contemporary training happens in institutional educational settings. Non-institutional training may be subdivided into that offered by two major stakeholders in translation: professional bodies and the industry itself.

Most countries have at least one association which brings together professional translators with the aim of jointly defending their interests, promoting the profession and ensuring standards. The vast majority of these organize professional development programmes for members, normally in the form of short courses designed to deal with very specific aspects of translators' work: new technologies, marketing, tax, copyright, terminology management, revision, and so on.

Similarly, some of them organize longer-term programmes such as the American Translators' Association (ATA) **mentoring** scheme, whereby senior experienced professionals offer guidance to novices over a period of time, facilitating their entry into the profession. This association also has a **Continuing Education** programme whereby member must earn a minimum of 20 points every three years in order to maintain their **accreditation**.

> Which professional translators' associations exist in your region or country? Have a look at their website to see what kind of training activities they organize. Do they have a mentoring scheme or similar?

Industry and training

Larger translation companies run short **staff development** courses, and longer initial training for recent recruits. SDL International, for example, runs a six-month training programme covering essentially technological aspects of professional translation and localization. Many also have agreements with universities whereby they offer **work placements** to advanced level students, allowing them to acquire on-the-job experience to complement more academic training.

> Which are the major translation companies in your area? Do they offer training programmes for recruits? With what content? Do they have arrangements for student work placements which your students will able to make use of?

Academic associations

Academic associations and societies in the field of translation studies are mostly devoted to research issues, but as training has been a much researched subject in our field and many researchers are also translator trainers, most have an interest in it. Many have training committees, for example; this is the case of large international associations such as EST or IATIS, as well as many national societies. These committees organize seminars, offer bibliographical data, and promote research into the training of translators in general. As such their activities are of interest to all translator trainers.

> Have a look at the website of the European Society for Translation Studies (EST), or the International Association for Translation and Intercultural Studies (IATIS). In what way do they organize their interest in training? Do they offer resources of interest to you as a trainer?

What about your national or regional academic associations, where these exist? Do they have a body which deals with training issues? In what way? Could their activities be of use or interest to you?

Major approaches to translator training

Early training approaches

For a long time in the history of translator training, trainers have assumed that students or apprentices learn to translate simply by translating. As professional translators with little time to devote to reflection on how to organize teaching and learning, many early trainers limited class activity to asking for on-sight (oral) translation of journalistic and literary texts, with little or no prior preparation on the part of the students, and to offering their own "correct" version as a model after public confirmation that the students' versions lacked professional quality. This approach to training was essentially apedagogical, and of course extremely frustrating for students. Fortunately, translator training has evolved, not only alongside Translation Studies as a discipline and alongside Linguistics (with the consolidation of text linguistics, discourse analysis, pragmatics, for example), but also with educational approaches in general (consolidation of student-centred paradigms as opposed to the **teacher-centred transmissionist** tradition). It is, however, still possible to find variations on the traditional model in translator training courses today. In the following few pages, we will give an of necessity brief overview of the evolution which has taken place, through reference to major authors and their approaches to training.

The importance of establishing teaching objectives: Delisle

The basic educational premise of establishing clear **objectives** for any teaching/learning process was probably first applied to translator training by the Canadian scholar Jean Delisle, as late as 1980. In his first major publication *L'analyse du discours comme méthode de traduction* (1980), he offers a systematic proposal for a practical introductory course in English-French translation, for which he suggests 23 teaching objectives. In his second major publication on training, *La traduction raisonnée* (1993), he distinguishes between **general** and **specific objectives**. There are eight of the former in his proposal (1993: 16):

- Metalanguage of translation for beginners
- Basic documentary research skills for the translator
- A method for translation work
- The cognitive process of translation

- Writing convention
- Lexical difficulties
- Syntactic difficulties
- Drafting difficulties

These proposals are accompanied by a wide range of class activities, proposed for each of the many specific objectives listed. In a later article (Delisle, 1998), suggests using **Bloom's taxonomy** (see Chapter 2) for the formulation of teaching objectives, instead of the nominal formulation he uses in 1993.

Delisle's translational approach is informed by the *théorie du sens*, and also partly by the Canadian contrastivist tradition of Vinay and Darbelnet, despite his criticism of their work. But his essential contribution to translator training had little to do with this theoretical aspect of his work; it was rather to remind trainers of the need to apply basic teaching principles to their classes, one of the most important being the establishment of clear and achievable objectives, in line with the systematic approach adopted in this book. In his opinion, this key element in planning offers the following four major advantages:

- It facilitates communication between teachers and students
- It facilitates the choice of teaching tools
- It suggests different learning activities
- It provides a basis from which to assess learning (Delisle, 1998: 21-2)

Towards profession-based learner-centred approaches: Nord
Nord (1988/1991) proposes a very complete model for translator training, based on the premise that training should simulate professional practice, that is, it should never involve translating without a meaningful realistic purpose, unlike many of Delisle's rather more contrastive-linguistic activities. The proposal is centred on a translation-orientated and functionalist model for text analysis, whereby students answer the following questions borrowed from New Rhetorics in order to facilitate realistic translation tasks designed to develop translator competence.

Who
        is to transmit
to whom
what for
by what medium
where
when
why
        a text
with what function?

> *On what subject matter*
> > is he to say
> *what*
> *(what not)*
> *in which order*
> *using which non-verbal elements*
> *in which words*
> *in what kind of sentences*
> *in which tone*
> *to what effect?* (Nord, 1991: 144)

She goes on, in this and other later publications, to offer detailed considerations and very practical advice on curricular design, selecting materials, texts, progression, class activities, student motivation or assessment, among others, making her undoubtedly one of the most exhaustive authors on the subject. Her approach is a clear move towards student-centred teaching/learning, and towards professional realism in the classroom, paving the way for more recent approaches in this vein. It is important to underline, however, that Nord's approach emphasizes the gradual nature of the acquisition of translator competence, and the need for considerable teacher intervention, particularly in the early stages, to ensure that tasks are not only realistic, but also feasible and hence not de-motivating.

Process-centred approaches: Gile
Both Delisle and Nord insist on the importance of process for training, as opposed to the traditional tendency to emphasize the product, that is students' translations. In this view, training should insist on how to go about translating, and not on the actual written product of that complex process, as it is in mastering the process that future professionals gradually acquire professional expertise.

From this perspective, the work of Gile (1995) is interesting for several reasons.

- He combines considerations on translating and interpreting, underlining similarities between the two; most authors in Translation Studies limit their reflections to one of the two major modes of translation.
- Like Nord, he understands translating and interpreting as acts of professional communication.
- He deals with the issue of quality from a professional point of view.
- He deals in some depth with the question of documentary research for translating and interpreting.
- He offers a critical review of literature on translator and interpreter training existing at the time.

In his own words,

> The idea is to focus in the classroom not on results, that is, not on the *end product* of the Translation process, but on the process itself. More specifically, rather than simply giving students texts to translate, commenting on them by saying what is "right" and what is "wrong" in the target-language versions produced, and counting on the accumulation of such experience and indications to lead trainees up the learning curve, the process-oriented approach indicates to the student good Translation *principles, methods,* and *procedures*. (Gile, 1995: 10)

To this end, he proposes a series of models and basic concepts, some of which are: communication, quality, fidelity (to the message), comprehension and knowledge acquisition (documentary research); the models are the sequential model of translation, the effort model (for interpreting), the gravitational model (also for interpreting). Some of these are then applied to actual classroom activity, and some interesting and innovative exercises are proposed. Gile identifies the following advantages in a process-orientated approach.

- Progress is faster than with a product orientation, which is based on trial and error.
- Attention is focused clearly on one aspect of the process at a time, avoiding dispersion, whereas product orientation implies dealing with all the problems which arise at the same time.
- Greater emphasis is laid on translation strategies, allowing students better to assimilate how to work, rather than whether or not their efforts have borne fruit.
- Greater flexibility is possible in areas such as linguistic acceptability or fidelity, which is particularly useful in the early stages of training, when comparing students' results with the teacher's or with "ideal" versions can prove de-motivating or even conflictive.

He claims that this process-orientated approach is especially appropriate for the early stages of training, whereas in the later stages there is probably a need for more emphasis on product. It is interesting to note this progression, as few authors in fact suggest methodological changes as students progress: the tendency is to propose one approach and stick to it throughout training.

Cognitive and psycholinguistic research applied to training: Kiraly and others

Since the mid eighties, and particularly in the nineties, an empirical approach to the study of translation based on cognitive science has also found applications to the training of translators. Kiraly, initially one of its major authors, vouches for a "systematic elaboration of the issues underlying a descriptive translation pedagogy, a pedagogy based on the accurate theoretical description of translation practice." (1995: 3). In this, his first book he bases his findings on a think-aloud protocol study carried out with 18 subjects translating from German into English (out of their native language). This study gives rise to a tentative model of the translation process on which to base training (see Kiraly, 1995: 101).

One of the interesting elements of Kiraly's proposal, is the centrality in the model of what he calls the translator's **self-concept**; the development of this awareness of their role becomes a key aim of training. Similarly, by way of conclusion, he offers us the following considerations aimed at improving training programmes.

- Teaching should emphasize the acquisition of interlingual, intercultural and intertextual associations.
- Error analysis might be a significant teaching resource.
- Based on error analysis, teachers can provide guided practice to improve the acquisition of intuitive skills and then teach conscious strategies as methods for problem resolution and the production of translation alternatives.
- A major objective should be the fostering of a translator self-concept and a functioning translation monitor.
- As students advance, skills are less likely to be acquired by repeated practice; less likely to develop naturally without specific training and pedagogical intervention, and more likely to involve translation quality at levels beyond that of mere semantic and syntactic correctness.
- Training should reorganize around a theoretical framework that allows the identification of cognitive resources that translation students should acquire and the pedagogical tools for teaching and testing the acquisition of those skills and knowledge. (1995: 110-2)

A summary of the work of other authors working from a similar perspective can be found in Jääskeläinen (1998: 268). Also of interest are the collective monographs published by the TRAP (Translation Process) research group at Copenhagen Business School (Hansen 1999, 2002). Some of the findings with direct applications to training issues can be summed up as follows.

- Student translators tend to focus on the lexical transfer process.
- Professional translators focus on stylistic questions and the user's needs.
- Students are not aware of potential translation problems, whereas professionals' higher level of competence brings about greater awareness of these.

- Professionals' work moves from automatized processing in routine tasks to conscious processing in new situations.
- The translation process is not linear, but a constant coming and going between factors at macro- and micro-level, governed by an overall macrostrategy.
- Affective factors such as a positive attitude to their work and a high motivation level may form part of translator competence and even contribute to higher translation quality.
- Professionals use bilingual dictionaries to add nuance to meanings already established in their minds or to stimulate the search for solutions, whereas students depend on them to understand the source text.
- Professionals seem to apply the principle of minimum effort to their work, for example by correcting surface error as they go, or by monitoring stylistic quality at the final revision stage of the translation.
- Translators read texts in a different way to monolingual readers, conditioned by the task they are later to carry out.
- Translators show greater insecurity when translating out of their mother tongue.

The situational approach: Vienne, Gouadec

The **situational approach** to translator training is advocated by Jean Vienne (1994), to whom it owes its name. It is based on the idea that class activity should be made up of a series of translation tasks already carried out by teachers professionally, which means that they can play the role of initiator in the translation process in a more realistic way. In essence, this proposal is functionalist in its theoretical approach, but differs strongly from Nord's in that Vienne totally rejects the simulation of professional tasks alleging that "it is difficult, indeed sometimes impossible, to carry out a realistic analysis of the situation, and to answer the questions that might arise" (1994: 52). A further version of this proposal is that of Gouadec, who around the same date proposed incorporating real translation commissions for real clients into training programmes (1994; see also 2003). It is interesting to note that this idea is taken up by Kiraly in his second major publication on translator training (2000) (see below). Vienne's methodology consists of a situational analysis of the translation commission (not dissimilar to Nord's textual analysis for translation), in which the teacher acting as initiator replies to students' questions, thus giving them a framework within which to carry out the translation.

Task-based approaches: Hurtado, González Davies

In recent years, **task-based learning**, which has for some time been applied to foreign language learning and teaching (see for example Nunan, 1989), has been applied to translator training, particularly by Hurtado (1999) and González

Davies (2003, 2004). This approach is based on designing a series of activities,

> concrete and brief exercises that help to practice specific points [...] lead-
> ing along the same path towards the same end, or task [understood as] a
> chain of activities with the same global aim and a final product. On the
> way, both procedural (know-how) and declarative (know-what) knowl-
> edge are practiced and explored. (González Davies, 2004: 22-23)

This is an approach which advocates an overall **curricular design** based on **learning outcomes**, and as such when applied to translator training can be seen as a development of Delisle's first steps in this direction, and indeed, at least in part, an application of Biggs' systematic approach to aligned curricular design (2003) which we will consider later in this book. Both Hurtado and her team at the Universitat Jaume I de Castellón, Spain (1999) and González Davies, alone (2004) or with her team at the Universitat de Vic, Spain (2003), offer a rich variety of suggestions for class activities for different levels and kinds of trans-lator training within this paradigm.

Balancing conscious analysis with subliminal discovery: Robinson

Robinson offers his own personal approach to translator training in 1997, and in a revised second edition in 2003, under the learner-centred title *Becoming a Translator*, which incorporates an interesting balance between slow academic (conscious, analytical, rational, logical and systematic) learning on the one hand, and fast, real-world learning (holistic, subliminal). To underline the importance of speed of learning for Robinson, the first edition carries the sub-title: *An Accelerated Course*, interestingly changed in the second edition to: *An Introduction to the Theory and Practice of Translation*. The text is especially admirable in the way in which it covers professional, theoretical, personal, cognitive, semi-otic, social, cultural and linguistic sides of translation, forming a very complete and integrated whole for learners. From the training point of view, Robinson offers a well-founded discussion of learning, starting from the thesis:

> [T]ranslation is intelligent activity involving complex processes of con-
> scious and unconscious learning; we all learn in different ways, and
> institutional learning should therefore be as flexible and as complex and
> rich as possible, so as to activate the channels through which each stu-
> dent learns best. (Robinson, 2003: 49)

Of further interest, in the light of recent developments in higher education in general, is Robinson's concept of the professional translator as a life-long learner. Both editions of the book contain many very thought-provoking activities for readers to carry out both in class and in self-learning situations.

The socioconstructive approach: Kiraly

Finally, Kiraly in 2000 publishes his second major book on translator training in which he criticizes his own earlier work in the cognitive field and turns to **social constructivism** as his inspiration for an essentially **collaborative approach** to translator training. Essential elements continue to be the students' self-concept and their socialization into the professional community of translators, now through authentic translation practice (see the situational approach above). In Kiraly's words:

> [l]earning is best accomplished through meaningful interaction with peers as well as full-fledged members of the community to which learners are seeking entry. [...] Rather than attempting to build up students' translation-related skills and knowledge atomistically in simulated exercises prior to translation practice, it would be much more constructive to start each pedagogical event with a highly realistic, and if possible genuine, translation project. (2000: 60)

This approach has been understood to be antagonistic with the task-based approaches described above, although more recently authors such as Marco (2004) or Kelly (forthcoming) have interpreted the two as being compatible, and simply different points on a cline of student progress.

This chapter has offered a brief overview of the evolution of translator training from both an institutional and a methodological point of view. Readers are strongly recommended to read the work of the authors mentioned above, together with others also listed under further reading, in order to acquire a deeper and more personal understanding of each approach. In the following chapters, this book will draw on all the authors mentioned, to differing degrees and ends.

Further reading on institutional history and information

Caminade, Monique and Anthony Pym (1998) 'Translator-training Institutions', in Mona Baker (ed.) *Routledge Encyclopedia of Translation Studies*. London: Routledge. 280-5.

European Society for Translation Studies (EST): http://www.est-translationstudies.org

International Association for Translation and Intercultural Studies (IATIS): http://www.iatis.org

International Federation of Translators (FIT): http://www.fit-ift.org [With links to national and regional member professional translators' associations].

International Permanent Conference of University Institutes of Translators and Interpreters (CIUTI): http://www.ciuti.org [With links to member institutes].

Translator Training Observatory, Intercultural Studies Group, Universitat Rovira i Virgili, Tarragona, Spain: http://isg.urv.es/tti/tti.htm

Further reading on methodological approaches

Colina, Sonia (2003) *Teaching Translation. From Research to the Classroom*. New York, San Francisco: McGraw Hill

Delisle, Jean (1980) *L'analyse du discours comme méthode de traduction: Initiation à la traduction française de textes pragmatiques anglais, théorie et pratique*. Ottawa: Presses de l'Université d'Ottawa. [English translation of Part I by Patricia Logan and Monica Creery: (1988) *Translation: An Interpretive Approach*. Ottawa: University of Ottawa Press]

------ (1993) *La traduction raisonnée. Manuel d'initiation à la traduction professionelle de l'anglais vers le français*. Ottawa: Université d'Ottawa.

Gile, Daniel (1995) *Basic Concepts and Models for Interpreter and Translator Training*. Amsterdam: John Benjamins.

González Davies, María (coord.) (2003) *Secuencias. Tareas para el aprendizaje interactivo de la traducción especializada*. Barcelona: Octaedro-EUB

------ (2004) *Multiple Voices in the Translation Classroom*. Amsterdam: John Benjamins.

Gouadec, Daniel (2003) 'Position Paper: Notes on Translator Training', in Anthony Pym, Carmina Fallada, José Ramón Biau and Jill Orenstein (eds.) *Innovation and E-Learning in Translator Training*. Tarragona: Universitat Rovira i Virgili. 11-19. [Also available at http://www.fut.es/~apym/symp/intro.html or in N°. 1 of the journal *Across Languages and Cultures*].

Hurtado Albir, Amparo (dir.) (1999) *Enseñar a traducir. Metodología en la formación de traductores e intérpretes*. Madrid: Edelsa.

Kiraly, Donald (1995) *Pathways to Translation. Pedagogy and Process*. Kent, Ohio: Kent State University Press.

------ (2000) *A Social Constructivist Approach to Translator Education. Empowerment From Theory to Practice*. Manchester: St Jerome.

Kussmaul, Paul (1995) *Training the Translator*. Amsterdam: John Benjamins.

Nord, Christiane (1988) *Textanalyse und Übersetzen*. Heidelberg: Groos [English translation by Penelope Sparrow and Christiane Nord (1991) *Text Analysis in Translation. Theory, Methodology, and Didactic Application of a Model for Translation-Oriented Text Analysis*. Amsterdam: Rodopi].

Robinson, Douglas (1997) *Becoming a Translator. An Accelerated Course*. London: Routledge. [2nd edition 2003: *Becoming a Translator. An Introduction to the Theory and Practice of Translation*].

Vienne, Jean (1994) 'Towards a Pedagogy of "Translation in Situation"'. *Perspectives* 2 (1): 51-9.

2. Planning and Writing Objectives/outcomes

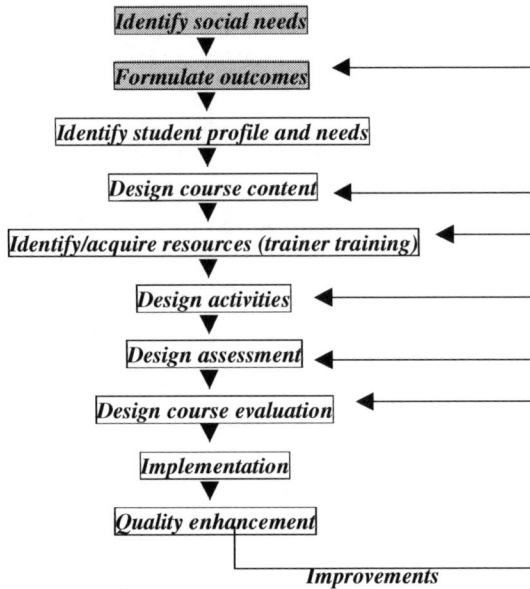

```
                    ┌─────────────────────┐
                    │ Identify social needs│
                    └─────────────────────┘
                              ▼
                    ┌─────────────────────┐ ◄──────────────┐
                    │ Formulate outcomes  │                │
                    └─────────────────────┘                │
                              ▼                            │
              ┌──────────────────────────────┐            │
              │ Identify student profile and needs│        │
              └──────────────────────────────┘            │
                              ▼                            │
                    ┌─────────────────────┐ ◄─────────────┤
                    │ Design course content│               │
                    └─────────────────────┘               │
                              ▼                            │
        ┌──────────────────────────────────────┐ ◄────────┤
        │ Identify/acquire resources (trainer training)│    │
        └──────────────────────────────────────┘          │
                              ▼                            │
                    ┌─────────────────────┐ ◄─────────────┤
                    │ Design activities   │                │
                    └─────────────────────┘                │
                              ▼                            │
                    ┌─────────────────────┐ ◄─────────────┤
                    │ Design assessment   │                │
                    └─────────────────────┘                │
                              ▼                            │
                    ┌─────────────────────┐ ◄─────────────┤
                    │ Design course evaluation│            │
                    └─────────────────────┘               │
                              ▼                            │
                    ┌─────────────────────┐               │
                    │ Implementation      │                │
                    └─────────────────────┘                │
                              ▼                            │
                    ┌─────────────────────┐               │
                    │ Quality enhancement │───────────────┘
                    └─────────────────────┘
                           Improvements
```

Summary and aims

This chapter deals with the outcomes of the training process. It may seem a little strange to start at the end, so to speak, but from the systematic approach to curriculum design used in this book, it is essential in designing any training process to establish first and foremost what we intend to achieve. By the end of this chapter, readers should be familiar with concepts such as teaching objectives/learning outcomes, **generic and specific competences**; **translation/translator competence**, and should be able to establish what professional translators of today need to know and to be able to do in order to fulfil their professional tasks in their own particular context; all of these concepts are useful in order to be able to describe accurately what the intended outcomes of a particular **programme** or **course** are, or should be. It is particularly important to stress that, although there are undoubtedly commonalities to the professional translator's situation and activity throughout the world, there are regional, national and cultural differences, as well as differences from one sector of the profession to another, which should be taken into account in the design of any specific training programme. This chapter will not, for that reason, actually propose one set of objectives/outcomes, but rather offer a broad framework within which teachers/trainers can design their own.

Curricular design and planning

In the words of Cannon and Newble,

> the key to curriculum planning is to forge educationally sound and logical links between planned intentions (expressed as objectives), course content, teaching and learning methods, and the assessment of student learning while taking account of student characteristics. (2000: 142-143)

In the chapters following this one, we will take what has been described as the systematic approach (D'Andrea, 2003: 29-30) to curricular planning and cover each of the elements in turn, starting – as stated above – at the end, or rather the intended end, of the process: its **aim**(s), and lower-level subdivisions of those overall aims, known as specific learning outcomes. The degree to which you are personally involved in this process as an individual teacher or trainer will depend to a great extent on the institutional and organizational context you are working in. In some university systems individual lecturers have little say in planning, particularly at the macro-level of overall course structure, but even at the micro-level of individual **modules**; in others, the design of modules depends almost exclusively on the individual lecturer, who may also have considerable say in the overall course design; in an **in-house training** context, you may be asked to design an entire short course yourself, or to run a course already designed in great detail by a training unit; in most contexts, there is some sort of academic planning committee or training unit which you can opt to join or may be appointed to at some point in your career.

In all of these cases, it is important for you to be aware of how decisions are taken, what your role may be in the process, and to be able to offer reasoned proposals when necessary. The more aware individual members of teaching staff or trainers are of how the curriculum has been designed, and perhaps more importantly, why it has been designed in that way, the more personally involved they will become in the process and the more effective a contribution they can make to the overall aims of the course.

> Think of your own present context, and the courses you are responsible for. How have they been designed at different levels (overall course structure; individual modules…)? Who designed them? What has been, is, or could be your role as an individual teacher or trainer?

Teaching objectives/learning outcomes

It may seem extremely obvious that the first step in any design process is to establish what we intend to achieve by implementing it. It is, however, the case that many training courses, especially those run in certain university systems and academic traditions, do not have explicit definitions of their intentions which can be referred to by both staff and students as a basic reference point. It has now for some time been recognised in most systems, as part of the general move towards improving student learning, that explicit intentions must be formulated for all courses. Early steps in this direction usually involved the writing of teaching objectives, i.e. what the teacher wanted the student to learn, with emphasis on teacher input. Currently, emphasis is being placed in many systems on learning outcomes, or what students will be able to do at the end of the course. Whichever point of view is prevalent in your context, it is most likely that courses are now required to be explicit and transparent about their objectives/outcomes.

Factors in defining intended learning outcomes (objectives)

Let us now move on to how we can go about defining our intentions, both at the level of overall aims and of lower-level subdivisions, i.e. specific learning outcomes/objectives. There are many different possible sources, depending once again on the context you are working in, these being a few of the most frequently important:

- social needs (often linked to the local or regional economy)
- professional standards (sometimes not expressed formally; in other cases, very clearly set out and broken down into component parts, as is the case of the UK National Standards by the Language National Training Organization: see full reference in further reading)
- industry's needs and views
- institutional policy (or corporate policy in the private sector)
- institutional constraints (national regulations or legislation; available training resources, etc.)
- disciplinary considerations (existing research and literature; common practice on other similar courses in your country or others)
- student/trainee profiles.

> Think again of your own context. Which of the above are particularly appropriate as sources for planning learning outcomes? Are there others not mentioned here which you have to take into account? Which?

One of the most important of these factors is beyond doubt the sociocultural and institutional context in which courses are to be offered. There is clearly a large difference between a full undergraduate or postgraduate programme at a state university, where there are general educational considerations to be taken into account, and a professional development course organized by a professional association or a short in-house induction programme at a large language service provider, where such considerations do not come into play at all. Similarly, for example, universities in systems with a strongly academic tradition will not formulate their overall aims in the same way as those with a more vocational tradition. One might indeed question whether the former would actually be interested in translator training programmes as such at all! Quite a different matter is the training of future TS researchers, although in practice in many cases these two very different aims are expected of the very same undergraduate programme, yet another consideration influencing the definition of outcomes.

> Which do you consider to be extra or special constraints on the overall intentions of your programme in your particular context? Think of institutional considerations (academic vs vocational; tertiary education as a public service, etc.) or resources, whether staff, technical or other (we will return to these in Chapters 3 and 5). How do these constraints affect the aims of the programme?

As institutional factors will vary tremendously from one context to another, we will not attempt to go into detail on them here, limiting our considerations to current general tertiary education trends, but rather we will try to stress other factors which are more likely to be common to the many different contexts you may be planning training for. In this chapter these may be summed up essentially in two broad areas: professional considerations (standards and opinions from future employers), and disciplinary considerations (existing research and literature in TS regarding training). In the next chapter we will go on to look in depth at both student profiles and teaching staff. This does not mean that the other factors are less important. Indeed, on many occasions they will be determinant in the decision-making process, but it would be impossible for us to cover all possible scenarios here. For an interesting, if controversial, case study in the analysis of institutional policy and academic politics as an allegedly decisive factor in curriculum planning in Translation in Spain, for example, see Pym (2000).

Professional considerations

If our overall aim is to train professional translators, a logical starting point would seem to be a description of what professional translators are actually required to do. This is one of the major starting points chosen by the **European Higher Education Area** in the **Bologna Process** currently underway to harmonize higher education throughout the European Union for the curricular design of higher education courses in general. Similar processes are taking place in higher education in other parts of the world, a point we will return to below in the section on competences or skills.

> Based on your own experience or knowledge of the sector, write a brief description of what you believe professional translators actually do in their daily work.

You may have found that such a seemingly simple task is not in fact as easy to fulfil as it may initially appear! Many authors agree that the profession has become increasingly complex and disperse in recent years, most particularly – although not exclusively – with the advent of new technologies. Let us now attempt to outline the essentials of the current state of the translation profession, with all the precaution that such an enormous task warrants. Compare the different points made with your own description.

A fairly standard reply to the question "what does a translator do?" is found in the following careers guidance description by the UK Languages National Training Organization (LNTO, today the National Centre for Languages, CILT) in a 2002 leaflet:

> Translators work with the written word. They convert documents from the source language into the language of the people who need to know and read the content of the translation (ie the target language) and the final translated document should read as clearly as it did in the original. (http://www.cilt.org.uk)

This simple description is of course open to all kinds of criticism and comment. Let us examine some of them: the text assumes, contrary to much contemporary practice (multilingual documentation, for example), that there is always *a* source text. It further assumes that the source and target texts are both in entirely written mode, thus excluding a wide variety of new (and not so new) textual forms (audiovisual or multimedia texts of all kinds, including software, for example); and that the target text is always *needed* by the reader. Translation is described as taking place between languages; and the final dictum on the clarity of the target text and its relation to that of the "source language document" would be questioned by much professional practice (where source texts are often of poor quality and standard translation practice is to improve on it), and indeed falls foul of some contemporary translation theory (where ease of reading of the target text is sometimes criticized as strongly domesticating). Perhaps a more useful and up-to-date description of the profession would take bi- and multilingual text production as its core element. This obviates (as do many authentic professional situations) the need for an actual source text as such; and allows for the inclusion of increasingly frequent multimedia text forms. It also avoids normative statements which may or may not be of application to specific professional situations.

Another way of approaching the current state of the field is through analysis of job advertisements and descriptions: let us consider the following job advertisement for translators in a large international language service provider or the official European Commission job profile for translators below.

SDL INTERNATIONAL

SDL International, one of the leading localisation companies with offices globally, are currently recruiting high calibre, dynamic individuals for the following positions. SDL's clients include Microsoft, Corel, Disney, Kodak amongst other blue chip companies.

Permanent Spanish IT Translators – Ref. SP_Uni2000

To be responsible for the translation of software, on-line help, Web Sites, documentation, games, as well as testing of localised products and linguistic advising in studio recordings.

The successful candidates should meet the following requirements:

- Spanish mother tongue speaker
- Educated to degree level, preferably with a qualification in Translation (English)
- High level of computer literacy
- Familiarity with translation memory tools such as Trados
- High level of interactive and communication skills
- Detail-oriented and quality-focused

In addition to a unique opportunity for career development in an international and very challenging environment, SDL offers a competitive salary, pension, salary continuation, life assurance and private medical insurance.

Please send your CV to:
Alison Cracknell, SDL International, Butler House, Market Street, Maidenhead, Berkshire, SL6 8AA, Fax: +44 (0)1628-410505

Email: acracknell@sdlintl.com quoting the Ref Number.

Figure 2. Advertisement for a translator position in SDL International
(reproduced with permission)

Translators with the Commission are required to translate, normally into their first language, texts of a political or legal nature that are frequently complex and encompass all the European Union's areas of activity (economic, financial, scientific, technical, etc.).

The **basic profile** we look for in our recruits is that of high-calibre graduates with an appropriate qualification in any scientific or arts discipline relevant for the work of the EU-institutions, and the capacity to adapt and evolve professionally to meet our basic requirements. These requirements are:

- an ability to grasp varied and often complex issues, to react swiftly to changing circumstances, to manage information and to communicate effectively;
- an inclination to show initiative and imagination, and to maintain a high degree of intellectual curiosity and motivation;
- a capacity to work consistently and under pressure, both independently and as part of a team, and to fit into a multicultural working environment;
- an ability to operate under administrative rules of the type applicable to a large public-service organisation.

In addition to these basic requirements, which apply to all Commission recruits regardless of their specialisation, our recruitment profile focuses on graduates who have – or are prepared to acquire – the **specific skills** set out below, and are willing to upgrade these and other skills throughout their term of employment.

Language skills
- Perfect command of all aspects and stylistic levels of the first language.
- Thorough knowledge of two or more other languages, preferably English, French or German, or – if only one of those – of that language plus one of the other official EU languages.

Thematic skills
- Familiarity with economics, financial affairs, legal matters, technical or scientific fields.

Translation skills
- A capacity to understand texts in the source language and to render them correctly in the target language, using the register and other language conventions that correspond to their intended purpose.
- A capacity to obtain rapidly and efficiently, in both source language and target language, the background knowledge (facts, terminology, language conventions) necessary to produce a translation of professional standard, even in less widely known fields. This includes the ability to use research tools and to become familiar with research strategies.

* A capacity to master computer-assisted translation and terminology tools, as well as standard office-automation software.
http://europa.eu.int/comm/dgs/translation/workingwithus/recruitment/translator_profile_en.htm

Finally, reflections by leading professionals and theoreticians add further elements to our analysis. An interesting description is that of Shreve in 2000, reflecting precisely on the evolution of the profession:

> The profession of translation [can be seen as] a special kind of ecosystem moving through time, modifying itself under the pressure of influences emanating from its socio-cultural environment, and evolving successfully from one form into another. (Shreve 2000: 217)

The constant evolution evoked here is, I believe, essential to any description of professional activity in our age. Not in vain is one of the essential concepts of current education policy that of lifelong learning in recognition of the impossibility for educational institutions clearly to define the future needs of society in concrete terms, and thus the need to prepare trainees to be flexible, adapt and constantly learn new skills.

Shreve goes on to mention in his text the dispersion of the language industry (which, he claims, has replaced and subsumed the translation profession) into many different professional roles often taken on by graduates trained as translators: bilingual editors, multimedia designers, research and information specialists, cultural assessors, multicultural software designers, software localizers, terminologists, and project managers (Shreve, 2000: 228).

Similarly, Kingscott (2000: 227) speaks of "a growing fragmentation" of the field. He further identifies as changes in the profession and trends for future developments: the globalisation of communication; the increasing use of English as a "world auxiliary language"; the changing pattern in the importance of other languages; translation becoming part of documentation and no longer regarded as a separate activity; the steady expansion of the use of language technology; and finally the multimodal nature of much text production.

As we have seen, then, there is an enormous range of activities and hence of skills required, and yet, they all belong to what is broadly termed the translation profession. This is clearly a problem for training courses, except in the case of a minority of very specialized courses designed to train specialists in only one area of translation expertise. Generalist courses, the vast majority of training courses the world over, have to try to cater for this huge diversity in the current market, while at the same time foreseeing likely future developments students should be prepared for.

> Compare the various activities described in the job advertisement and profile above and the comments by Shreve and Kingscott with your own description of translation activity in your context. Bear in mind that although there are common elements, your curricular design will depend largely on your own context, firstly in terms of aims and target employment market, and secondly in terms of educational structures.

If we are to describe our overall aims in terms of what professionals are required to do and to know, we need to be able to systematize the common denominator of what translators actually do in their daily work. This question has normally been addressed in Translation Studies under the somewhat controversial term or concept of translation or translator competence, which we will now go on to examine.

Disciplinary considerations

The following is a brief summary of what some authors in TS have said about translation competence. It has no pretension to being exhaustive, choices having been made from the existing literature to illustrate the wide range of differing proposals which have been drawn up, in a range of geographical contexts. Those chosen are presented here in chronological order, showing how the debate has evolved, and how (some of) the proposals have mutually influenced each other.

Wilss (1976: 120) suggests that a translator should have three competences, in an interesting early description of translation competence for curricular design purposes. It is interesting because it outlines several points which are later to be developed by others:

a) a receptive competence in the source language (the ability to decode and understand the source text)
b) a productive competence in the target language (the ability to use the linguistic and textual resources of the target language)
c) a supercompetence, basically defined as an ability to transfer messages between linguistic and textual systems of the source culture and linguistic and textual systems of the target culture.

Delisle (1980: 235), in the conclusion to his seminal work on translation pedagogy (see Chapter 1), identifies what he defines as four major essential competences: the linguistic, encyclopaedic, comprehension and re-expression competences. Roberts (1984: 172), also in Canada, offers the following five-point description:

1) linguistic [competence] (ability to understand the source language and quality of expression in the target language)
2) translational (ability to grasp the articulation of meaning in a text and to transfer it without deforming it into the target language, avoiding interference)
3) methodological (ability to document themselves on a given subject and to assimilate the corresponding terminology)
4) disciplinary (ability to translate texts in certain basic disciplines such as economics, computing, law)
5) technical (ability to use different translation aids, such as word processing, terminology data bases, dictaphones, etc.) [my translation from the French original]

It is interesting to note that Delisle himself (1992: 42) later accepts this version by Roberts, and underlines her substantial coincidence with Nord (1988/1991).

In one of the major works by the functionalist school of translation, not least because it is one of the first to be published in English, rather than German (see Chapter 1), Nord (1988/1991) claims that:

> ...the essential competences required of a translator [are] competence of text reception and analysis, research competence, transfer competence, competence of text production, competence of translation quality assessment, and, of course, linguistic and cultural competence both on the source and the target side. (1991: 235)

Pym (1992 and more recently in 2003) distinguishes between knowledge shared by translators and other professionals: grammar, rhetoric, terminology, world knowledge, common sense and commercial strategies; and what he calls "the specifically translational part of their practice", which is neither linguistic, nor common, nor commercial, but rather for him consists of two abilities:

– The ability to generate a target-text series of more than one viable term (target text$_1$, target text$_2$... target text$_n$) for a source text.
– The ability to select only one target term from this series, quickly and with justified confidence, and to propose this target text as a replacement of source text for a specified purpose and reader. (1992: 281)

Gile (1995:20) does not use the term translation competence, but does offer a description of what he terms "components of translation expertise": passive command of passive working languages; active command of active working languages; sufficient knowledge of subject matter of texts and speeches (elsewhere he uses the term "world knowledge"); knowing how to translate.

Hurtado (1996: 34) offers the following list of five subcompetences: linguistic competence in two languages; extralinguistic competence; analysis and synthesis; "translational" competence; professional competence.

Hatim and Mason (1997: 205) propose a model of, in their terms, "translator abilities", based on Bachmann's model of linguistic competence (1990), and the discourse perspective of the authors, in which three different areas of skills are contemplated: source text processing skills, transfer skills and target text processing skills.

Campbell, writing on translation into the second language (1998: 154) suggests a model based on three competences: target language textual competence, disposition, and monitoring competence, outlined after empirical research with a group of Arabic-speaking translation students working into English in Australia; the author himself recognizes the need to incorporate other elements into the model, which he considers provisional. In his conclusions, Campbell formulates four basic principles relating to translation competence models:

1. Translation competence can be separated into relatively independent components, and those components can be used as building blocks in curriculum design.
2. Translation education is a matter of intervention in the development of the various components of translation competence.
3. Students are likely to attain different levels of achievement in the various components of translation competence given the imbalance in their bilingual skills.
4. The assessment of translation quality is best seen as a matter of profiling the competence of learners, rather than simply measuring the quality of their output. (1998: 163)

Neubert (2000: 6) proposes the following classification, which he himself defines as "approximate": linguistic; textual; specific subject area; cultural; and transfer competence. As additional and original points of interest, he further suggests that the competences are interrelated, and that the overall competence is characterized by its "complexity, heterogeneity, approximation, open-endedness, creativity, situationality, and historicity" (2000: 5).

In recent and ongoing research, the PACTE group at the Universitat Autònoma de Barcelona in Spain has developed a model of translation competence, drawing on previous work by Hurtado, Presas and Beeby, all currently members of the group, among others. The six subcomponents of translation competence are defined as:

• communicative competence in the two languages
• extra-linguistic competence

- professional instrumental competence
- psycho-physiological competence
- strategic competence and
- transfer competence, these last two being central and governing all the others. (PACTE, 2000:101)

This proposal is interesting in that, like Neubert's, it establishes explicit interrelations between the different components, but differs in suggesting that these may be hierarchical in nature, situating transfer and strategic competence at a higher level than the others.

As we can see from this brief overview, although there is a level of agreement on some of the components of translation competence, particularly on the need for linguistic knowledge, there is an incredible variety of conceptual and terminological approaches.

Which, if any, of the descriptions do you consider to be most useful for the purpose of designing a training curriculum? Why?

Some of the controversy surrounding the concept of translation/translator competence lies with the term itself. We have already seen that some authors avoid it altogether, preferring "abilities", "components of expertise", or others. The concept itself is also used for multiple purposes. Campbell (1998: 6) suggests three main uses for the concept in TS:

a) the development of psychological models of the translation process;
b) the summative evaluation of the quality of translations as products (he is very critical of what has been done so far in this application);
c) the training of translators.

And, indeed, different authors have used the concept in these different ways: some in an attempt to describe the actual translation process as an expert activity from a cognitive perspective, whilst others have used the term from an educational point of view in a way similar to that adopted frequently by curricular planners today in many parts of the world. It is probably the case that these different applications have unnecessarily complicated the debate surrounding competence.

Some criticisms (see Mayoral 2001a, for example) underline the fact that the catalogue of subcompetences, subcompetencies or components of the macrocompetence (note the range of terms!) has not been empirically proven. This criticism is undoubtedly pertinent if the authors using or proposing the catalogue are claiming to describe the actual cognitive process of translating. If, however, they intend to provide a list of skills which a training course should provide, then the criticism would seem to be less well founded. Any direct or indirect observation (such as the one we have just carried out above) of the profession will quickly yield a series of skills which are currently required of recruits. Similarly, recent more formal surveys of employers have given information on what they expect translators to be able to do, thus providing empirical data, not on the cognitive process, but on the current demands of the sector. This procedure is in keeping with current curricular planning practice, and seems easily justifiable. Not to provide a detailed list of objectives as a starting point for the development of a training course on the grounds that insufficient empirical research has been carried out to sustain the proposal seems to me to be neglecting the very obvious point that translators are today enrolling on courses the world over, and that these courses can only work if they are clear on what their objectives are. Whether or not that list of objectives or intended outcomes uses the term "competence" seems secondary.

Taking into account the professional and disciplinary considerations above, I would suggest that the following is a useful list of areas of competence desirable in graduates from translation courses for the purpose we are interested in here, that of curricular design. The list may require completion with further elements in some contexts, depending on the role of training programmes, the areas may overlap on occasion to some extent, and each of the areas can of course be subdivided to differing degrees, depending on how specific our definitions of aims, objectives or outcomes need to be.

- Communicative and textual competence in at least two languages and cultures. This area covers both active and passive skills in the two languages involved, together with awareness of textuality and discourse, and textual and discourse conventions in the cultures involved.
- Cultural and intercultural competence. Culture here refers not only to encyclopaedic knowledge of history, geography, institutions and so on of the cultures involved (including the translator's or students' own), but also and more particularly, values, myths, perceptions, beliefs, behaviours and textual representations of these. Awareness of issues of intercultural communication and translation as a special form thereof is also included here.
- Subject area competence. Basic knowledge of subject areas the future translator will/may work in, to a degree sufficient to allow comprehension of source texts and access to specialized documentation to solve translation problems.
- Professional and instrumental competence. Use of documentary resources of all kinds, terminological research, information management for these

purposes; use of IT tools for professional practice (word-processing, desk-top publishing, data bases, Internet, email...) together with more traditional tools such as fax, dictaphone. Basic notions for managing professional activity: contracts, tenders, billing, tax; ethics; professional associations.

- Attitudinal or psycho-physiological competence. Self-concept, self-confidence, attention/concentration, memory. Initiative.
- Interpersonal competence. Ability to work with other professionals involved in translation process (translators, revisers, documentary researchers, terminologists, project managers, layout specialists), and other actors (clients, initiators, authors, users, subject area experts). Team work. Negotiation skills. Leadership skills.
- Strategic competence. Organizational and planning skills. Problem identification and problem-solving. Monitoring, self-assessment and revision.

The concept of competences in higher education and training

We shall continue to use the term *competences* in the remainder of this book, despite the controversy in TS on the issue, for several reasons set out here. Firstly, we do not intend in any way to offer a model for the cognitive process of translating, limiting our concept of competence to that of intended learning outcomes, thus hopefully avoiding much of the confusion outlined above. Secondly, it does still seem to be the preferred term in TS. Thirdly, it is the preferred term, on the whole, in current higher education and training research, and particularly in the European Higher Education Area. Fourthly, it is a wider concept than that of skills, also often used in educational contexts. A recent EU working group progress report by the Basic skills, entrepreneurship and foreign languages Working Group for the implementation of Education and Training 2010 defends the choice in this way: "*Competence* was considered to refer to a combination of skills, knowledge, aptitudes and attitudes, and to include disposition to learn as well as know-how" (2003: 10).

Much, and perhaps nowadays most, translator training takes place at universities on undergraduate and postgraduate courses of different kinds. These major contexts thus merit some specific attention in the next few pages; many of the considerations put forward will also have some application to other training contexts (in-house training; professional associations' continuous education and professional development courses, for example).

There has been a recent move in European higher education, and also in other parts of the world, toward a new model of tertiary education, where the key elements are clear definition of aims and intended outcomes and more student-centred learning. This move, together with an attempt to harmonize European curricula to facilitate graduate professional mobility with Europe and to make European higher education more competitive in the world, has led to a (hopefully) fruitful period of self-analysis and reflection in many tertiary education institutions. Clearly, translator training units, whether they be schools, faculties, departments or whatever, must take part in this overall movement and, indeed, have a great deal to contribute to the debate and analysis, for several reasons, not least of which is that as a discipline we have always shown a strong interest in training as a preferred area for research. It is the case that as an essentially vocational discipline, we have put much collective thought and debate into how best to train future professionals, which is not necessarily the case of other less clearly vocational fields.

The current debate also has a lot to offer TS. Let us consider here the concept of competences as part of this reform process, and see how it applies to our field, bearing in mind the brief discussion of the concept in TS above. Distinction is made between general, generic or transferable competences on the one hand, and subject area specific competences on the other. The first should be the aim of all undergraduate or postgraduate courses, the second only of those in their own field. The first form part of the tertiary education sector's mission to help individuals attain personal fulfilment and development, inclusion and employment; the second play a role more specific to their own respective fields.

With regard to this two-fold classification of competences, a striking idiosyncrasy of our field's is the way in which as a discipline we offer access to a very wide range of generic competences which I believe it is difficult to find today in other academic fields at university level. In this sense, if we take the list of generic competences as outcomes for undergraduate programmes drawn up as a basis for the work of the pilot Tuning project in the EU (see Figure 3 below), and compare it with the definitions of translation (hence subject-specific) competence above, we discover that our graduates are almost uniquely qualified as flexible, adaptable and highly employable citizens. This strong point of our training is something we should be aware of, as the incredible proliferation of translator training courses in numerous countries in recent years does now mean that many graduates from our courses will not work professionally as translators, thus implying that we could run the risk of training people with highly specialised competences which would not then be of use to them personally on graduation. The applicability of many of our subject area specific competences to other fields, that is their transferability, means that this risk is substantially reduced.

Overall aims

After our brief review of the professional, disciplinary and general higher education considerations, but most particularly taking into account your own input regarding your own professional, institutional or organizational context, you

---

Generic competences (González and Wagenaar, 2002)

Instrumental competences
Oral and written communication in the native language
Knowledge of a second language
Capacity for analysis and synthesis
Capacity for organization and planning
Basic general knowledge
Grounding in basic knowledge of the profession
Elementary computing skills
Information management skills (ability to retrieve and analyse information from
    different sources)
Problem solving
Decision making

Interpersonal competences
Critical and self-critical abilities
Teamwork
Interpersonal skills
Ability to work in an interdisciplinary team
Ability to communicate with experts in other fields
Appreciation of diversity and multi-culturality
Ability to work in an international context
Ethical commitment

Systemic competences
Capacity for applying knowledge in practice
Research skills
Capacity to learn
Capacity to adapt to new situations
Capacity for generating new ideas (creativity)
Leadership
Understanding of cultures and customs of other countries
Ability to work autonomously
Project design and management
Initiative and entrepreneurial spirit
Concern for quality
Will to succeed

Figure 3. Generic competences as defined in the EU Tuning Project

should now be able to broach the writing of objectives or outcomes for the programme or course you are designing. Objectives or outcomes should be formulated for all levels of planning: for overall programmes or courses, for individual course modules, for individual class sessions or **units** of teaching material. They can also be formulated with differing degrees of detail. It is standard practice to formulate firstly an overall aim, and then detailed individual outcomes. One might suggest, for example, that the overall aim of a full undergraduate course in translating at a state tertiary education institution is to train professional translators; that is of course an over-generalizing statement which in fact says very little. Notice also that it is formulated from the perspective of the teacher or the institution, rather than from that of the student. The overall outcome of such a programme could better be formulated thus:

> *On completion of the course, students will have acquired the necessary set of competences (knowledge, skills and attitudes) to be able to join the translation profession in any of its specialized areas in this country or abroad at a junior level.*

Would this formulation be valid for your situation? If not, explain why, and then write an alternative.

Writing clear learning outcomes is the first essential step to communication between teacher or institution and student, between trainer and trainee, so thought and care should be put into it. The basic rule is that outcomes should be easy for the student or trainee to understand; they will normally be written from the student's point of view, and in the future tense. Outcomes should also be realistic (achievable for students) and assessable (see Chapter 8). Remember that they are the basis for course content, teaching and learning methods and assessment of student learning. It is similarly important to remember that objectives/outcomes should give a clear indication of the level of achievement aimed at in each case.

For this purpose, most authors recommend some form or adaptation of Bloom's taxonomy of learning levels (1956), originally centred on the cognitive domain (and much criticized for this), but later extended by Bloom himself and other researchers to what they have called the affective, psychomotor, perceptual, experiential and interpersonal domains. We reproduce here, as an example, the "suggested words for outcome level statements (cognitive domain)" based on Bloom given by D'Andrea (2003: 35). Other authors offer similar suggestions; the lists are not intended to be exhaustive, but rather indicative of the kind of verbs which are appropriate for the textual genre "learning outcomes".

Level	Suggested words
Evaluation	Judge, appraise, evaluate, compare, assess
Synthesis	Design, organize, formulate, propose
Analysis	Distinguish, analyse, calculate, test, inspect
Application	Apply, use, demonstrate, illustrate, practise
Comprehension	Describe, explain, discuss, recognize
Knowledge	Define, list, name, recall, record

Figure 4. Suggested words for outcome level statements (cognitive domain)
based on Bloom (D'Andrea, 2003: 35)

A more recent alternative taxonomy of learning outcomes, considered by many to be more appropriate is SOLO, or Structure of the Observed Learning Outcomes (Biggs and Collis, 1982), and consists of five different levels of response in ascending order of complexity in both quantitative (learning more) and qualitative (learning better) terms: prestructural, unistructural, multistructural, relational and extended abstract. Biggs himself proposes the following hierarchy of verbs to form curriculum objectives:

Phase	Level	Verbs
---	Prestructural	Misses point
Quantitative	Unistructural	Identify Do simple procedure
	Multistructural	Enumerate Describe List Combine Do algorithms
Qualitative	Relational	Compare/contrast Explain causes Analyse Relate Apply
	Extended abstract	Theorize Generalize Hypothesize Reflect

Figure 5. A hierarchy of verbs for curriculum objectives
(adapted from Biggs, 2003: 48)

The following are some examples of possible overall aims for different levels of planning.

* Overall aims of a professional development course on translation memory technology:

At the end of the course, participants will be familiar with the principles of translation memory technology, be able to use at least one of the most common commercial programmes on the market, and to appreciate its application to their professional practice.

• An introductory course module on legal translation:
At the end of the module students will be able to identify the most salient features of legal texts, situate translation commissions in their legal and social context, identify documentary sources for their translation, and produce translations of highly conventionalized legal texts from language(s) X into language(s) Y.

• A teaching unit midway through an introductory module to translation:
By the end of this unit, students will be able to identify documentary sources other than dictionaries of use to the translator, understand how to use them efficiently, and evaluate their accessibility and reliability in different translation situations.

Write the overall aim(s) for:

❑ An in-house staff development course on revision technique for newly promoted senior translators taking on revision of other translators' work for the first time as part of their professional remit.
❑ A semester-long module on subtitling for a postgraduate programme on audiovisual translation.
❑ A teaching unit on medical terminology to be included in the initial stages of an advanced level module on scientific translation on an undergraduate translation programme.

Specific learning outcomes

Moving on to more specific learning outcomes, let us return to our full undergraduate training programme as an example. I suggest above that, on the basis of the review of sources carried out, we can identify the following main areas of competence for translator training in the context of a general higher education institution:

• communicative and textual competence in at least two languages and cultures;

- cultural and intercultural competence;
- subject area competence;
- professional and instrumental competence;
- attitudinal (or psycho-physiological) competence;
- interpersonal competence;
- strategic competence.

It is in general recommended that around five or six and no more than seven or eight specific outcomes be formulated in each case and for each level of planning. Based on this, specific learning outcomes for the area of interpersonal competence on a full undergraduate programme, for example, might be:

By the end of the programme:
- *Students will be able to identify, describe and analyse the different interpersonal relations which intervene in the translation process;*
- *Students will be able to work cooperatively with the different professionals who intervene in translation activity (fellow translators, revisers, documentary researchers, terminologists, layout specialists, editors), identifying the potential difficulties involved in each situation, and designing strategies for dealing with them;*
- *Students will be able to work cooperatively as professionals with other actors involved, such as customers, initiators, commercial intermediaries (agencies, etc.), authors, users, or subject area experts, identifying the potential difficulties involved in each situation, and designing strategies for dealing with them;*
- *Students will be able to justify to others the decisions they have taken during translation, appraise those of others involved in the process and communicate their opinions in such a way as to avoid or resolve potential conflict;*
- *Students will appreciate the advantages and potential pitfalls of cooperative work, and be prepared to avoid or resolve conflict.*

Comment on the applicability of these specific outcomes to your own context. Which are applicable? Which not? Why?

Now choose another area of competence from the list above, and write five or six specific learning outcomes for a full undergraduate programme. Try to bear your own context in mind when writing the outcomes.

Remember that the outcomes we plan and write will be the basis for the remainder of our curricular design: course content (in the widest sense), teaching and learning methods and the assessment of student learning. Following our systematic approach, the next few chapters will move on from here to examine the other elements involved in curricular design: students and staff; course content; resources; teaching/learning method and activities; sequencing; assessment of student learning and course/programme evaluation.

Further reading on professional standards

Languages National Training Organization (LNTO) (2001) *The National Standards in Translating.* London: LNTO.

Further reading on translation/translator competence

Campbell, Stuart (1998) *Translation into the Second Language,* London and New York: Longman.

Delisle, Jean (1998) 'Définition, rédaction et utilité des objectifs d'apprentissage en enseignement de la traduction'. In Isabel García Izquierdo and Joan Verdegal (eds.) *Los estudios de traducción: un reto didáctico.* Castellón: Universitat Jaume I. 13-44.

Hatim, Basil and Ian Mason (1997) *The Translator as Communicator,* London: Routledge

Hurtado Albir, Amparo (1996) 'La enseñanza de la traducción directa "general". Objetivos de aprendizaje y metodología'. In Amparo Hurtado Albir (ed.) *La enseñanza de la traducción.* Castellón: Universitat Jaume I. 31- 56.

Kelly, Dorothy (2002) 'La competencia traductora: bases para el diseño curricular'. *Puentes* Nº 1. 9-20.

Neubert, Albrecht (2000) 'Competence in Language, in Languages, and in Translation'. In Christina Schäffner and Beverly Adab (eds.) *Developing Translation Competence,* Amsterdam: John Benjamins. 3-18.

Nord, Christiane (1991) *Text Analysis in Translation. Theory, Methodology, and Didactic Application of a Model for Translation-Oriented Text Analysis,* Amsterdam: Rodopi; English Translation of Nord, Christiane (1988) *Textanalyse und Übersetzen.* Heidelberg: Groos.

PACTE (2000) 'Acquiring Translation Competence: hypotheses and methodological problems of a research project'. In Allison Beeby, Doris Ensinger and Marisa Presas (eds.) *Investigating Translation,* Amsterdam: John Benjamins. 99-106.

Pym, Anthony (1992) 'Translation Error Analysis and the Interface with Language Teaching'. In Cay Dollerup and Anne Loddegaard (eds.) *Teaching Translation and Interpreting. Training, Talent, and Experience,* Amsterdam: John Benjamins. 279-290.

------ (2003) 'Redefining Translation Competence in an Electronic Age'. In Defence of a Minimalist Approach. *Meta* XLVIII, 4. 481-497.

Roberts, Roda (1984) 'Compétence du nouveau diplômé en traduction'. In *Traduction et Qualité de Langue. Actes du Colloque Société des traducteurs du Québec/*

Conseil de la langue française, Québec: Éditeur officiel du Québec. 172-184.

Wilss, Wolfram (1976) 'Perspectives and Limitations of a Didactic Framework for the Teaching of Translation'. In Richard W. Brislin (ed.) *Translation Applications and Research,* New York: Gardner. 117-137.

Further reading on competence in general and learning outcomes

Biggs, John (2003) *Teaching for Quality Learning at University. What the Student Does.* Maidenhead: Open University Press [2nd edition. See especially Chapter 3 "Formulating and clarifying curriculum objectives".]

------ and Kevin F. Collis (1982) *Evaluating the Quality of Learning: The SOLO Taxonomy.* New York: Academic Press.

Bloom, Benjamin (1956) *Taxonomy of Educational Objectives Handbook I: Cognitive domain.* New York: McGraw-Hill.

D'Andrea, Vaneeta-Marie (2003) 'Organizing Teaching and Learning: outcomes-based planning'. In Heather Fry, Steve Ketteridge and Stephanie Marshall (eds.) *A Handbook for Teaching and Learning in Higher Education. Enhancing Academic Practice.* London: RoutledgeFalmer. 26-41.

González, J. and R. Wagenaar (2003) *Tuning Educational Structures in Europe. Final Report. Phase One,* Bilbao: Universidad de Deusto. Also available at: http://www.relint.deusto.es/TuningProject/index.htm.

Gosling, David and Jenny Moon (2001) *How to Use Learning Outcomes and Assessment Criteria.* London: Southern England Consortium for Credit Accumulation and Transfer (SEEC).

3. Participants in the Training Process: Trainees and Trainers

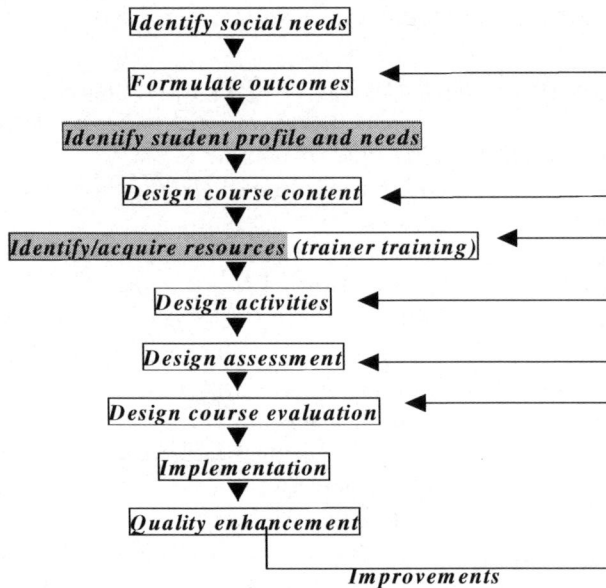

```
            Identify social needs
                   ▼
           Formulate outcomes          ◄──────────────┐
                   ▼                                    │
       Identify student profile and needs              │
                   ▼                                    │
          Design course content      ◄─────────────────┤
                   ▼                                    │
   Identify/acquire resources (trainer training)  ◄─────┤
                   ▼                                    │
           Design activities         ◄─────────────────┤
                   ▼                                    │
          Design assessment          ◄─────────────────┤
                   ▼                                    │
        Design course evaluation     ◄─────────────────┤
                   ▼                                    │
            Implementation                              │
                   ▼                                    │
         Quality enhancement ─────────────────────────┘
                        Improvements
```

Summary and aims

Moving forward in our systematic approach to curricular design from the planning of outcomes to the next important stage, this chapter will look at the participants in the process. The first, and most important, group of participants are the students or trainees. We will review the main factors to take into account in our curricular design: prior knowledge, personal characteristics, **learning styles**, expectations and **motivation**, degree of homogeneity, and consider how these factors affect our decision-making. Secondly, we will turn to the other main group of participants in the learning and teaching process: the teachers or trainers. Again, we will consider their prior knowledge and experience, **teaching styles**, expectations and motivation, together with the importance of coordination and team work on complex training programmes. By the end of the chapter, readers should be familiar with all these concepts, with TS literature on the issues involved, and identify those characteristics of participants which have an influence on curricular design in their own particular context.

Students/trainees

By far the single most important element in any training process is the trainee or learner. After spending quite some time on the intended outcomes of your course, your "finishing line", in the previous chapter, we shall now move "back" to your starting point. What do students know when they join your programme, course or module? If you are halfway through a programme, what modules have they taken previously? What modules are they taking simultaneously? How old are they? Are they full-time or part-time students? Do they have any special needs? What kind of teaching and learning environment are they accustomed to? Individually, which learning styles do they prefer? Why are they taking this course? What do they expect to learn, or to get out of the experience? How homogeneous or heterogeneous a group do they form?

Some of this information should be available at your institution or organization in the form of statistical data, or may be deduced from the context, but clearly much of it is specific to programmes, modules and individual students, and needs to be collected for each occasion. This process is known as **needs analysis** or initial diagnosis and is essential to any curricular planning process at any level. Much planning has to be done in advance and thus cannot initially take into account the individual needs of students, which has to be done through flexible application of your course design when it is actually finally implemented with a specific group of students.

> How much information on the students or trainees who will take your course do you have access to in your institution or training context? What kind of information is available? What will you have to find out for yourself? Note some ideas on how you might go about doing so.

Prior knowledge

This is the area most teachers and trainers focus on when describing student or trainee groups. It is far from being the only element which should be taken into account, but it is certainly an important one. In higher education, there is often a tendency to set unrealistic, idealized starting points for courses, presupposing much more prior knowledge than most students actually have. There is a frequently heard complaint amongst university lecturers that new students have less and less prior knowledge every intake. (A parallel may be found in the translation profession, where those responsible for recruitment complain bitterly about how little recent graduates know, often losing perspective with respect to what they themselves were able to do upon graduation.) It is hard to believe that these complaints have any serious grounding in reality in a world which offers much more, and much more easily accessible, information than ever before. What is probably true is that students do not know the same things as earlier generations did, and teachers and institutions have not adapted. And university education is now open to a much larger section of the population than before, inevitably moving away from previously elite (and memory-based) standards. It is indeed possible that average students entering higher education in many countries have less declarative knowledge of memorized facts than in the past, but they probably have much greater procedural knowledge of, for instance, how computers work than the vast majority of their teachers. It is also much more likely that they will actually have seen previously distant phenomena and realities through television, the cinema and the Internet. Or that they will have travelled outside their own region and country and thus have hands-on experience of the wider world.

Even if this were not the case, it would not be particularly useful to dwell on what students do not know, or what they used to know, since the teacher's task is to design courses for *these* students *today* (or tomorrow). What is important is to realize that students lacking the prior knowledge designated as necessary for any learning process will find progress difficult, if not impossible, and will rapidly become frustrated and de-motivated, reducing even further their likelihood of learning. Similarly, students who know much more than is initially planned for will become bored and equally de-motivated to learn. Finding a "happy medium" at the planning stage and being flexible at the implementation stage are thus two key factors for success. Let us look at the planning stage.

For the overall planning of an undergraduate degree, students' prior knowledge will depend to a great extent on the major secondary education system feeding into universities, and on higher education regulations regarding admissions procedures. In Spain, for example, most secondary school pupils still study only one foreign language, which this makes it impossible for university translation courses to require or assume prior knowledge of two foreign languages at advanced level as is the custom in many other countries. In France, national legislation establishes free entry to university for all students who have successfully completed secondary education; no further entry requirements or tests are therefore permitted. Most national systems have explicit indications of the outcomes levels for official national pre-university examinations. This kind of general context allows us some idea of the overall prior knowledge (in language(s) and other areas) of new students. It may, occasionally, allow us to intervene to establish specific levels or requirements over and above general university entrance criteria.

Secondary education outcomes
In your country or context, how many languages do students study in secondary education? To what level? Are the final years of secondary education highly specialised in very few areas ("Anglo-Saxon" tradition),

or are they more generalist (baccalaureate tradition, for example) in their design? What are the implications of your answers for the prior knowledge of students entering an undergraduate programme in translation in your context?

University entrance
In your country or context, is university entrance open to all those who successfully complete secondary education? If not, what are the selection criteria usually applied for university entrance? What are the implications of your answers for students' prior knowledge on entering an undergraduate programme in translation in your context?

If translation is normally taught at postgraduate level in your context, what are the criteria for admission, and what are the implications for the prior knowledge of students?

What are the advantages and disadvantages, respectively, of entrance examinations or admission tests for translation programmes?

In this general discussion, we have paid particular attention to language knowledge or proficiency, but the need to identify prior knowledge in other areas is of course also important. For example, in a context in which computer use is not widespread amongst the population in general or at pre-university education levels, a course in translation will probably include an introductory module designed to facilitate the acquisition of basic keyboard and computer skills; in countries with widespread access to computers at home and at school such a module would make little sense, and more time would be devoted to advanced skills and specific applications. The same applies to other areas such as cultural or area studies, general writing skills and so on.

For specific modules within undergraduate programmes, some idea of prior knowledge may be gleaned from analysis of the place of the module on the overall course structure. In which year of the course is the module taught? Which modules have been taken prior to it? What are the intended outcomes of those modules? Similarly, colleagues who have taught the earlier modules are a very useful source of information on actual class groups, their progress and performance. Often, institutions have official committees or other bodies where this information is shared with colleagues. It is also important to remember that students will usually be taking other modules simultaneously, and will thus also gradually bring other learning to the classroom.

Outside higher education, participants in short professional or in-house training courses may have a very wide range of prior knowledge. Such courses are often limited to one specific aspect of translation practice (translation memory tools; billing and tax; terminology management…), to few participants at a time, and are usually flexible in their design. This may make identifying (or establishing criteria for) prior knowledge easier on occasion, but it is certainly the case that less institutional contextual information will be available and that most of the information on the prior knowledge (and other characteristics) of participants will usually have to be gathered *ad hoc* for this kind of course.

> In your context, what information is readily available on students' prior knowledge before joining your module or course? Note the different sources you can think of for this information.

Whatever amount of information you can collect at the planning stage of your course design, it is important to remember that you will still need to gather information on the actual class group you teach on each occasion. This may be done in a variety of ways which we will return to at the end of this section on students.

Personal characteristics

It is a fact that the student population in higher education generally and worldwide is becoming increasingly heterogeneous. There are several reasons for this, notably including internationalization and greater access to higher education for groups previously excluded or under-represented, such as women, older learners or students with special needs due to disability. This means that it is essential for teachers to be aware of the make-up of each student group and how it may influence class activities. In particular, older students may approach learning in a different way, as may students from other countries. We will go into more detail on the issue of learning styles in the next section.

Outside the typical context of full higher education programmes at undergraduate and postgraduate level, the rapid changes today's society is undergoing and will continue to undergo mean that the traditional idea of a university degree preparing professionals for their whole careers is no longer applicable, and has been replaced with the concept of lifelong learning. This means that more people than ever before are currently engaged in some form of continuous training or education, also in the field of translation, leading to increasingly heterogeneous groups of trainees and of training situations.

> On which personal characteristics of the student/trainee group do you think you need to have information in order to design your course appropriately? How can you obtain this information?

How do you think a personal characteristic such as student age should influence your course design?

Where can you obtain information on support resources for students with disabilities at your institution or organization? Will their presence affect your course design? How?

Learning styles and approaches

The increasingly heterogeneous composition of student groups in higher education has probably made teachers more aware of different learning styles, though these exist and have always existed even in the most apparently homogeneous groups. Although there has been much recent research into learning, it is still the case that knowledge about learning processes is limited, and in particular that it is difficult to draw detailed conclusions on implications for teaching. In this section we will consider briefly some of the findings on which there is substantial consensus, or which may be of special interest for translator training. Those interested in more detailed reviews of current research should refer to the further reading section at the end of the chapter.

The first and most important premise is that not everyone learns in the same way, and in particular that not everyone learns in the same way as the teacher does! Students' individual characteristics and personalities, and their prior educational background and culture influence the way they learn, as does the interaction between their individual learning styles and teachers' teaching styles. Although learning styles are not generally believed by researchers to be unchangeable, they are often very deeply rooted, and thus may be difficult to change.

The second premise, taken from constructivist theory, is that learning takes place when changes or additions are made to pre-existing knowledge and understanding, constituting a process of individual transformation. Social versions of constructivist theory take a less individual and more collective view of learning as the achievement of understanding within a community of practice.

The third is that we learn through experience, gained in a variety of contexts and ways. Perhaps the most influential description of this experiential learning process is what is known as the Kolb learning cycle. As you can see in figure 6, this cyclical process moves from concrete experience (doing) to reflective observation (reflecting) to abstract conceptualization (forming principles) to active experimentation (planning), and back to concrete experience. For effective learning to occur, learners must move through all four stages of the cycle, although individual preferences probably mean that learners dwell more on particular stages than others.

Do
(*Concrete experience*)

Plan
(*Active experimentation*)

Reflect
(*Reflective observation*)

Form principles
(*Abstract conceptualization*)

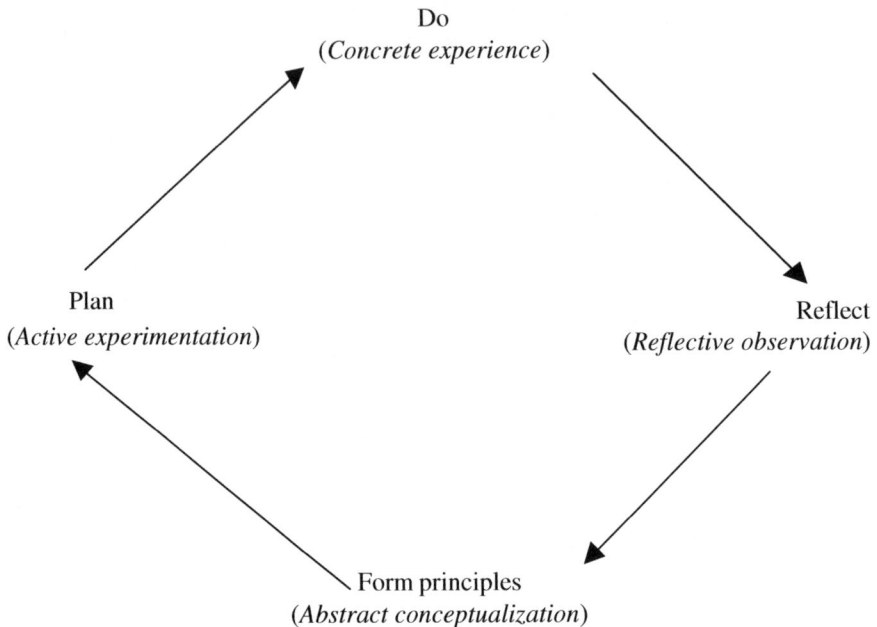

Figure 6. The Kolb or experiential learning cycle

On a slightly different level, research in the 1970s and 1980s (Marton, 1975 or Marton and Säljö, 1984) first suggested that the quality of learning depends on what have been called learning approaches, of which two were originally identified. The surface approach to learning, normally motivated by extrinsic factors such as a need to pass an examination, consists in fulfilling the task at hand, often by memorizing facts, with little or no analysis and little or no engagement with the meaning of the task. The outcome of this kind of strategy is typically low quality learning which remains at only superficial levels of cognitive processing (which does not necessarily mean low examination marks!). The deep approach, on the contrary, implies meaningful engagement with the task, critical evaluation, reaching high levels of cognitive processing (although not necessarily the memorizing of data!). This kind of approach is normally associated with intrinsic motivation, such as strong interest in the subject. The two approaches are probably better understood as two extremes on a continuum. A third approach, identified by Biggs (1987), is known as the strategic approach, and involves the same learner swapping from a deep to a surface approach normally in function of assessment and the need to obtain high grades at a particular point in the learning process. It has been postulated that traditional didactic approaches (including rote learning) lead to the surface approach, while experiential learning and other constructivist approaches lead to the deep approach and higher levels of understanding.

To sum up, current research (see further reading) would seem to indicate that students are more likely to reach higher levels of understanding and adopt a deep approach to learning when the teaching and learning environment allows for the following: intrinsic motivation; active involvement in realistic learning tasks; independence and choice; cooperative work; a challenging, but supportive and low-threat environment; frequent and constructive feedback; practice and reinforcement; all this within a well organized and structured framework with emphasis on higher-level objectives (understanding) (Cannon and Newble, 2000: 9).

Expectations and motivation

As we have just seen, current research clearly points to motivation as a crucial factor for the success of learning processes. It follows, then, that teachers and course designers must be aware of student expectations and motivations when choosing to join a translation course. Research into measuring student motivation has been less abundant than in other fields of educational research, but some has been done. Studies carried out in the UK (Newstead et al., 1996) indicate that students give essentially three kinds of reason for choosing university courses (and this is at least partially applicable to other training contexts): the most frequent is what the authors have called "means to an end", that is the **extrinsic motivation** of improving their standard of living, improving their chance of finding a good job; this is followed by "personal development", the **intrinsic motivation** of fulfilling personal potential, improving life skills and gaining control of their own life, gaining knowledge for its own sake or furthering a particular academic interest. The third kind of reason identified has subsequently been defined by the authors as "amotivation" or lack of motivation: this is the "stop gap" group of reasons: avoiding the world of work, taking "time-out", having fun and so on. Newstead and Hoskins (2003) now suggest that there are two scales involved here: one is degree or strength of motivation, a continuum from amotivation to high achievement motivation (desire to succeed). The other is a classification of kind of motivation: from purely intrinsic (learning for learning's sake) to purely extrinsic (the desire to find a good job or acquire high social status). Both are movable scales, and it would seem that strength of motivation is probably more important than the nature of the motivation itself, although research results to date are inconclusive.

Elements which have been identified as important for student motivation once on a particular course are: amount and kind of feedback; assessment systems; perceptions of the department, university, or even the university system in general (Newstead and Hoskins, 2003). Let us comment briefly on each. Students investing a great deal of time and effort in tasks only to find that there is little reward and less explanation as to why will rapidly become de-motivated. Positive, constructive and individual feedback is, thus, essential. This is closely related to assessment systems, many of which encourage surface approaches and rote learning in order to achieve high grades. A variety of assessed tasks, and particularly assessment systems designed to show higher levels of conceptual understanding, and encourage use of knowledge in problem-solving are more likely to lead to deep approaches to learning, and to maintain motivation (see Chapter 8 for further discussion of assessment techniques). Negative student perceptions of the department, university or university system are especially difficult to tackle, as of course these are large institutional systems and as such resistant to change (Biggs 1993); individual students (and members of staff!) may lose initial motivation if they perceive that as individuals their role is insignificant. It is evident that moves to more student-friendly environments at different levels within institutions may help to modify perceptions of this kind and hence encourage motivation.

Let us now attempt to analyse briefly the question of student motivations for joining translator training courses. As for most courses, there is a variety of reasons for students choosing to join. The most obvious would seem to be that they want to become professional translators; this is perhaps a major motivation for postgraduate contexts where students have already achieved a basic level of university education (often in modern languages), and perhaps realized that in order to find a good job with relative ease they need more specialized training. On undergraduate courses, however, this very specific motivation may in fact be less frequent than expected. Some students will have a very clear idea that they want to be translators or interpreters, usually in international organizations, attracted by the glamour which surrounds this kind of elite environment; but they are often a minority. Research currently underway at Spanish universities (Calvo, forthcoming) suggests in fact that many students are motivated by a desire to study in the general field of modern languages, but also by a rejection of traditional university courses perceived as too narrowly academic and lacking in future employment opportunities. That is, many students entering first year of undergraduate programmes do not necessarily want to become professional translators and may not even be very sure what a professional translator does, but rather want to study something related to languages, which will help them to find an interesting job often defined as "not as a language teacher". Other motivations given by students include a desire to travel, or even what we could call academic "fashions". Translation may be a new, innovative, fashionable thing to study, or may be perceived as a prestigious course because students joining it tend to have very good academic records or because entrance requirements are very demanding.

On short professional or in-house training courses, the motivations tend to be extrinsic and very specific: in order to do their job better, faster, more safely, more profitably, translators perceive a need to use a new IT tool, to know more about civil liability insurance, to get to know more about the translation of new text types (multimedia), or to add a new language combination to their repertoire. The strength of these motivations is usually also high, as there is less external (family, social) pressure to join courses of this kind than to acquire a first degree or a first job, and the initiative usually originates in the translators themselves.

> What do you believe are the main motivations of students/trainees joining your course? Are they intrinsic or extrinsic in nature? How strong do you think they are? How do you think they might affect student/trainee learning?

As in other matters, there will be an enormous variety of replies to these questions. The key element is once again to adapt decisions to your own context.

Degree of homogeneity

We have already mentioned above that student groups at university are becoming increasingly heterogeneous, essentially due to internationalization and to the inclusion of groups previously excluded from or seriously under-represented in higher education. This is true of undergraduate and postgraduate courses in many countries throughout the world. Short professional courses will also draw highly varied trainee populations, due amongst other reasons to the heterogeneity of the profession as a whole.

> How homogeneous a group do you expect to find on your course? If you expect a heterogeneous group, what kind of diversity do you expect to find? How might it affect your course design?

One particularly noteworthy factor in this increasing heterogeneity of student groups at university is that of international mobility programmes. In many parts of the world, universities, national authorities and international organizations have set up programmes designed to promote student and staff mobility, often but not exclusively on an exchange basis. Thanks to the Erasmus programme, for example, it is not unusual to find student groups with seven, eight or more nationalities in university classrooms throughout Europe. This major change in the composition of student groups is here to stay, and is generally welcomed by university staff as an enriching experience for all involved. It is surprising, however, just how little has been done to take this new situation into account in course design. The tendency is for the "visiting" student to "sit in" as a kind of privileged observer, but rarely as an active participant in teaching and learning processes at the host institution. Moreover, staff often complain that exchange students change the nature of their classes, for example by upsetting the directionality of translation class activities; another reaction is to claim that they cannot really be taken into account because they are only taking a limited number of modules and not the entire course (see Mayoral and Kelly, 1997 for a more detailed discussion). Of course it is true that each exchange student will only be at the host institution for a semester or a year at most, but it is no less true that there will in all probability always be a group of exchange students on our courses, and that these programmes will continue to exist and indeed to grow. Taking *all* students into account in both course planning and implementation is a basic premise for quality teaching and learning (see Tsokaktsidou, 2005).

> To what extent does your institution participate in international mobility programmes? Do you expect to have international exchange students on your course? In what proportion with home students? From which countries? Will this affect your course design? What kind of problems do you expect these students to face? Are they different from home students' problems? Does exchange students' presence affect the directionality of class activities? How might you deal with this?

Needs analysis

At several points in this discussion of student profiles we have mentioned needs analysis as an effective tool for teachers. Some data is available within institutions in a variety of forms, including:

- statistical data on where students took secondary education
- statistical data on student origin
- statistical data on previous grades obtained by the class group or individual students
- feedback from other teachers who have worked with the group
- standards for secondary education outcomes
- learning outcomes from previous modules taken by the group.

These sources are useful, but will not give you a complete picture of what your students already know, what they expect from your module, what has motivated them to join it (or the programme), or which particular needs they may have. Many teachers design their own needs analysis instruments which they use in the initial stages of the academic period, often the first day of class. These may take a variety of forms, including:

- short question and answer tests
- translation exercises or similar
- questionnaires (varying in length and complexity)
- short essays on motivation and expectations
- class debates on expectations
- buzz group discussions followed by reports back to the plenary session (see Chapter 6 for further explanation of this kind of activity).

Which form you decide to use will depend on your own particular module, programme and maybe academic tradition (some students prefer to debate, others to write, for example). It is, however, important for your planning to include a list of characteristics you need to know about the students taking your module, and a clear plan for how you are to obtain this information.

Taking into account this discussion of student profiles, write a list of the characteristics of your students you need to know more about in order to adapt your planning to their specific needs (prior knowledge, personal characteristics, learning styles, expectations and motivation, degree of homogeneity, etc.).

Now note for each point on your list how you intend to obtain the information you need. Where the students themselves are the source, think carefully about how you will obtain the information from them in each case, and decide which kind(s) of instrument you need to design.

Teachers/trainers

The other major group of participants in the teaching and learning process is that of the teachers or trainers. It may be convenient to comment at this point that some authors associate the use of the term *teacher* with traditional teacher-centred didactic approaches, and for that reason prefer *educator* or *facilitator*. My use of the term does not imply such an approach, it is simply the standard term used in a multitude of situations and the most easily understood in most cases.

In this section we will be dealing mostly with those whose major occupation is teaching. There may be considerable differences with the many people who occasionally teach on short courses, but whose major occupation is another, whether it be translating, localizing, interpreting, managing or writing, although some of the considerations will be equally valid for both groups.

It is probably the case that the majority of those involved in translator train-ing are full-time university lecturers. This fact has many implications for training, not least that full-time university lecturers are expected to carry out a large number of other tasks which are not directly linked to training as such. Most university systems expect full-time lecturers to be quite heavily involved in research, and often reward (by promotion, for example) dedication to and achievements in research much more than in teaching, which seems inevitably to take second place. Many university lecturers also have heavy administrative or management responsibility at different levels, as heads of department, as course leaders, as exchange coordinators, as work placement tutors, and so on. Much of this work is essential if courses are to offer a wide variety of learning opportunities, and teaching staff usually have a better understanding of the implications of this kind of activities for learning than purely administrative staff or management. This encourages many teachers to become involved in these activities, often despite little recognition from the institution. Whatever the system, it is hard to find teachers who only teach.

> In your context, what proportion of their working hours do teachers spend on teaching and related activities: tutorial and student support work, pre-paring classes, designing courses and materials, marking work or student monitoring? What proportion do they spend on other activities? How does your institution view the relative importance of each activity? Is promotion linked to good teaching? How is good teaching rewarded?

After this brief initial comment and turning to our field, in most TS litera-ture about training, much is written in general terms about processes and activities, but much less about the people involved, whether they be students or teachers. What has been written about teachers (with very few honourable ex-ceptions) focuses mainly on their prior knowledge and experience; as in the case of the students, we turn firstly to this issue.

Prior knowledge and experience
We have already noted that university lecturers are expected to carry out a large number of tasks, and indeed these tasks are often directly related to the require-ments they have to fulfil in order to be employed initially in most systems. That is, new members of the teaching staff will usually be highly qualified in the discipline, normally with a postgraduate or doctoral qualification, indicating research competence. In some systems prior teaching experience will be viewed positively; in others short training programmes in teaching are offered for those who do not have teaching experience or competence. TS literature, however,

normally indicates professional experience as a translator as being the essential prerequisite for successful teaching. The following three quotes deal with the issue from different angles, but all in essence make the same demand of the translator trainer: professional translation experience.

> It cannot be expected that language instructors without professional translation expertise will have a professional translator self-concept themselves or that they will be able to help their translation students develop one. (Kiraly 1995: 3)

> [In reply to "How should trainers be trained?":]
> Another simple answer to a simple question: teachers on a translator-training programme should spend one month in all three of the following situations:
> – Working in a translation firm (either as a translator or a reviser or a terminologist)
> – Working in an in-house translation service (same as above)
> – Being a free-lance professional (same as above).
> That should be enough for a start. And that should clearly determine on their teaching approaches. (Gouadec 2003: 13)

> It is certainly enriching for students at translation schools to have professional translators as teachers, but this is not without its problems: professional translators lack specific training. (Durieux 1988: 8) [my translation from the original French]

Analyse each of the three quotes and consider your own personal opinion on this matter.

Are you a professional translator? If so, have you had any teacher training? Will your institution offer you training? If you are not a professional translator, how can you become familiar with the professional world you are training students for?

Do you share the view that professional translation experience is a must for a teacher on a translation course? Why (not)?

Whatever your personal opinion on this matter, the fact is that your institution will normally require you to be a productive researcher, and/or to participate in administrative or management tasks alongside your teaching. Our discipline will require you to have professional translation experience either prior to or simultaneous with your teaching. That is, a lot of very varied demands involving very varied competences and skills are going to be made on you all at once. In this section and in this book in general we are going to focus only on teaching competence, but the other demands will continue to be present, and cannot be neglected. The view we will adopt from now on is that, irrespective of other considerations, those devoting themselves to teaching or training should first and foremost be professional teachers and trainers. Paradoxically, however, universities have traditionally paid little attention to teacher training. In many systems, compulsory training exists for all other levels of education, but at universities it is simply assumed that those who know, know how to teach. Fortunately, some university systems are now introducing initial and continuing training programmes, but it is still the case in many countries that new members of teaching staff are left literally to sink or to swim. This book is intended to alleviate some of the anxiety that situation can produce!

Teaching styles

Just as students have learning styles, teachers have teaching styles or approaches, which they have learned, acquired or developed through experience, or from models (often teachers from their own time as students) of what to do, or what not to do. Research suggests that the interaction of teaching and learning styles has a strong effect on outcomes, with some teaching styles encouraging surface learning approaches, and others encouraging deep learning.

> Take a moment to think how you see your role as a teacher. Describe briefly your obligations in the teaching and learning process as you see them. Now describe briefly your students' obligations.
>
> Now consider the list of characteristics given in figure 7 below. On each line, mark the statement closer to your own personal preference or belief.

It is unlikely that you will have situated all your answers in either one of the two columns. Most of us as teachers will have found statements closer to our own personal beliefs in both. There is, however, probably a tendency to find more answers on one side of the table. If you have more replies in the left-hand column, your approach to teaching and learning is more teacher-centred; if you have more answers in the right-hand column, then your approach is more student-centred. Research suggests that student-centred approaches are more likely to produce quality outcomes, that is higher level learning and understanding. In the following chapters we will give suggestions as to how more student-centred approaches may be incorporated into translator training, into the design of materials and activities, and into assessment systems. Some of the suggestions may not be applicable to some contexts. The pretension of this book is not to give one-size-fits-all solutions, but rather to provide food for thought and proposals designed to help improve translator training, by careful adaptation to each training context, student population and, importantly, teacher population.

Most or all decisions regarding content and method should be made by teachers	Choices regarding content and method should be made partly or mostly by students
Emphasis (including responsibility for assessment) should be on individual subjects or course units	Emphasis (including responsibility for assessment) should be on the overall programme and its aims
The teacher is an expert who should transmit knowledge	The teacher should be an expert guide for students and facilitate their learning
The teacher transmits information	The teacher asks questions
Student activity should be mostly individual	Cooperative learning is more effective
Students learn in the classroom or in programmed activities	Students learn anywhere anytime
Achieving good marks and praise from teachers is a major motivation	Intellectual curiosity and personal responsibility are major motivations
Class arrangements should be planned beforehand and not modified	Class arrangements may, indeed should, be modified as the course develops
Assessment is the teacher's responsibility only	Self and peer assessment may be useful tools for learning
The most important outcome is for students to learn syllabus content	The most important outcome is for students to acquire learning techniques
Assessment should be summative	Assessment should be formative
The whole class group should progress together at the same pace	Individual students should progress at their own pace
All students should learn the same	Individual students may learn different things
Teachers work alone	Team work is an essential part of teaching
Teachers and individual departments or academic units should have autonomy	Teachers and academic units should work together in close collaboration

Figure 7. Views of teaching and learning
(adapted from Cannon and Newble, 2000 and Villa, 2004)

Expectations and motivation

Much as student motivation is a key factor in student learning, teacher and trainer motivation is also a key factor in the success of training programmes. De-motivated staff will be unable to encourage student motivation, forming a vicious circle. Beyond the intrinsic human motivation of wanting to help trainees to be successful in their future personal and professional lives, there are of course extrinsic factors, which often depend on institutional policy, and which are normally beyond the control of individual teachers: working hours and working conditions in general, salary scales, opportunities for promotion, recognition of quality teaching, a pleasant teaching team atmosphere. It is often the strength of intrinsic motivation which keeps teachers going; we can only try to ensure that institutions become increasingly aware of the importance of extrinsic factors to staff motivation and take steps to improve it!

> List aspects of your professional situation which you find motivating.
> Now list those you find de-motivating. Is it possible to rectify any of the
> latter? How?

Coordination and team work

Student-centred approaches are characterized by emphasis on overall programme aims, rather than on individual course units. In this respect there are very different academic traditions. In some systems teachers have sole responsibility for individual course units, including assessment, and students must pass all units in order to complete the overall programme (e.g. Spain) . In others, there is little obligation regarding what students must do and/or pass during the course, but rather emphasis is given to achieving overall competences, which are demonstrated in final examinations or assessments for the entire programme (e.g. Germany). In others, there are mixed systems, where individual units must usually be taken and passed, but some compensation is allowed between them, and an overall final grade is often awarded (e.g. United Kingdom, France). Each of these systems reflects a different view of what a course is or should be. There is no doubt that training in a complex activity such as translation must necessarily adopt a networked approach to course design, and that compartmentalization in hermetic course units should be avoided as far as possible. This implies a strong need for coordination and team work, preventing the sensation many students have today that there is no relation between different course units (Calvo, 2001), in practice rendering much effort invested in time and learning a lot less useful than it could be if approached from a more integrated perspective.

Team work, offering opportunities for rewarding interpersonal professional relationships, and saving on duplicated effort, is also usually a motivating element in a teacher's activity. This is particularly true of otherwise unpleasantly competitive academic environments.

> In your context, is emphasis given to overall programme aims or to indi-
> vidual course units? How is this emphasis materialized in practice (in
> assessment, in mechanisms for coordination...)? Does the current situa-
> tion encourage or discourage networked learning?

In this chapter we have reviewed the characteristics of the two major groups of participants in translator training: students and teachers, and commented on their influence on course design and implementation. We have insisted on the importance of taking these factors into account and adapting to the context in course planning, and of flexibility in the implementation of courses. Teaching and learning is an essentially interpersonal activity, and as such the significance of the roles of the different participants cannot be over-stressed. From here, we move on to the next step in curricular design: course content in the widest sense.

Further reading on students

Biggs, John (2003) *Teaching for Quality Learning at University. What the Student Does.* Maidenhead: Open University Press [2nd edition; see especially Chapter 4 "Setting the stage for effective teaching"].

Calvo, Elisa (2001) *La evaluación diagnóstica para la traducción jurídica. Diseño de un instrumento de medida.* Unpublished postgraduate dissertation. Universidad de Granada, Spain.

------ (forthcoming) *Desarrollo de la concepción académica y profesional durante los estudios de Traducción e Interpretación por parte del estudiantado.* Doctoral dissertation in progress. University of Granada, Spain. [information on both pieces of research available from calvoelisa@gmail.com]

Cannon, Robert and David Newble (2000) *A Handbook for Teachers in Universities and Colleges.* London: Kogan Page [Especially Chapter 1 "Helping students learn" and Chapter 2 "Student-centred learning"]

Carroll, Judith and Janette Ryan (forthcoming) *Teaching International Students.* London: Routledge.

Fry, Heather; Steve Ketteridge and Stephanie Marshall (2003) 'Understanding Student Learning'. In Heather Fry, Steve Ketteridge and Stephanie Marshall (eds.) (2003) *A Handbook for Teaching and Learning in Higher Education. Enhancing Academic Practice.* London: RoutledgeFalmer. 9-25.

Marchese, Theodore 'The New Conversations about Learning. Insights from Neurosciences and Anthropology, Cognitive Science and Workplace Situations'. Available from http://www.newhorizons.org/lifelong/higher_ed/marchese.htm

Newstead, Stephen E., A. Franklyn-Stokes and P. Armstead (1996) 'Individual Differences in Student Cheating'. *Journal of Educational Psychology* 88: 229-241.

Newstead, Stephen E. and Sherria Hoskins (2003) 'Encouraging Student Motivation'. In Heather Fry, Steve Ketteridge and Stephanie Marshall (eds.) (2003) *A Handbook for Teaching and Learning in Higher Education. Enhancing Academic Practice.* London: RoutledgeFalmer. 62-74.

Robinson, Douglas (1997) *Becoming a Translator. An accelerated course.* London: Routledge. [2nd edition 2003: *Becoming a Translator. An Introduction to the Theory and Practice of Translation.* Chapter 3, entitled "The Translator as Learner" is of particular interest for the points covered here.]

Tsokaktsidou, Dimitra (2005) *Los estudiantes de intercambio en el aula: una guía de buenas prácticas.* Granada: Universidad de Granada.

Further reading on trainers

Pym, Anthony; Carmina Fallada; José Ramón Biau and Jill Orenstein (eds.) (2003) *Innovation and E-Learning in Translator Training.* Tarragona: Universitat Rovira i Virgili. [Part I, pp 1-60 transcribes and summarizes an on-line symposium on translator training held in 2000, which contains some debate on who should train translators. The text is also available at http://www.fut.es/~apym/symp/intro.html or in N°. 1 of the journal *Across Languages and Cultures*].

4. Curricular Content

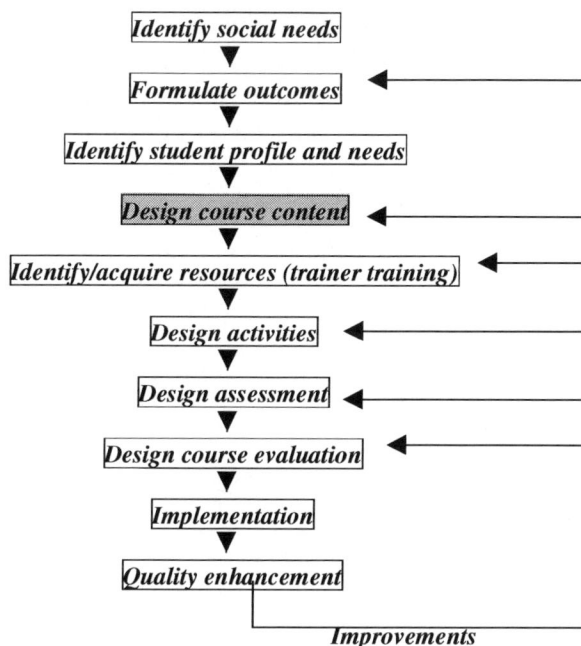

```
Identify social needs
        ▼
Formulate outcomes          ◄──────────────┐
        ▼                                  │
Identify student profile and needs         │
        ▼                                  │
Design course content       ◄─────────────┤
        ▼                                  │
Identify/acquire resources (trainer training)  ◄──┤
        ▼                                  │
Design activities           ◄─────────────┤
        ▼                                  │
Design assessment           ◄─────────────┤
        ▼                                  │
Design course evaluation    ◄─────────────┤
        ▼                                  │
Implementation                             │
        ▼                                  │
Quality enhancement                        │
        └──────────────────────────────────┘
            Improvements
```

Summary and aims

Now that we have dealt with learning outcomes and the people involved in your curriculum, we can move on to curricular content, the central issue in this chapter. Once again, we will not be proposing one single set of elements which are valid for all contexts, but rather intend to present different issues to be solved at the design stage and which will be strongly influenced by the context in which training is taking place. By the end of the chapter, readers should be able to identify the issues to be examined in deciding on curricular content, the factors influencing decisions, and to offer possible solutions for their particular contexts. Amongst the issues addressed are: academic versus vocational contexts; undergraduate versus postgraduate models; level of specialization, and core content. This will be approached partly through four case studies of actual programme outlines, one of which is analysed in detail. Finally, there is an overview of content organized in the major areas of competence described in Chapter 2.

Contexts

We went into some detail in Chapter 2 on the constraints which may be involved in different contexts for the establishment of objectives or intended outcomes for training courses. These same constraints, together with those arising from the characteristics of the people involved in the process (teaching staff and students) affect the next stage of planning: that of content design. Let us briefly run through some of the major elements influencing content selection before going on to examine a series of case studies of actual courses of different kinds, and to present some general considerations on the major areas of competence involved in translator training. It is important to indicate that by *content* we do not mean purely declarative knowledge-based elements, but rather a wide range of competences (knowledge, skills, attitudes) which are to be developed, consolidated or achieved.

Academic versus vocational
If we are working in an academic context, objectives and intended outcomes will probably be more general, covering more generic competences, than those of a purely vocational context, where the major aim is to for the student to acquire the specific professional competences required. This factor will have major impact on decisions such as how much theoretical content should be included in the curriculum.

Undergraduate versus postgraduate
If we are working at undergraduate level, students will normally be younger and will have less prior knowledge (for example of their working languages), less experience in general, and will also require development of a range of generic competences alongside the specific professional competences. National legislation in some countries may require particular content on undergraduate courses, whereas postgraduate courses normally offer much more leeway to the course designer.

Levels of specialization
Closely linked to the previous two points is the question of the degree of specialization. If we are planning to train highly specialized translators in one field (say, technical translation), content will clearly be determined by this option: there may be modules on types of technical text, technology in modern society, on technical terminology and its formation, with little or no attention being paid to issues such as the cultural and ideological implications of translation, which would, however, be fore-fronted on courses specializing in translation of literature or in the media. Specialization inevitably implies reducing breadth of content in favour of depth in one particular field. It is for this reason that specialized

courses tend to be found at postgraduate or professional level, whereas more general courses tend to be found at undergraduate level. Particular contexts will determine when and how specialization can be incorporated into the curriculum: in countries with undergraduate degrees in translation, postgraduate courses can afford to be highly specialized in one field (audiovisual translation; technical translation; legal translation; translation theory...), whereas those with general undergraduate courses in languages tend to offer less specialized postgraduate courses in translation in general. It is important to adapt to the context, both from this end (entering knowledge of students) and from the other: what does the market require of new translators? Is a high level of specialization required? In which fields?

Duration

All these factors influence and are influenced by the duration of the course. Within the European Higher Education Area, a full undergraduate course, for example, will last between 180 and 240 ECTS (European Credit Transfer System) credits, typically between 3 and 4 years' full-time study. Postgraduate courses last between 60 and 120 credits (1 to 2 years' full-time study).

Although they are not the only factors to be taken into account, these are certainly important factors for the design of our curriculum. Go back to the list you wrote in Chapter 2 when designing outcomes, and in the light of your own context, answer the following questions:

- Is your course academic or vocational?
- In what way does this necessarily affect course content?
- Is your course undergraduate/postgraduate/continuous professional development?
- What level of entering knowledge can you expect your students to have?
- What are market demands regarding degree of specialization?
- What legislative requirements exist in your country, region or context with regard to course content?
- How long will your course be?

Case studies

From the above it will be clear that there cannot be one proposal for core content for all translator training courses. It is, however, probably true that there are elements which will be present in the vast majority of initial training courses (whether they be undergraduate or postgraduate). These can be derived from the notion of translator competence which we developed in chapter 2, where we proposed the following areas of competence as fairly representative of what both the discipline and the professional translation market believe professional translators should possess:

- communicative and textual competence in at least two languages and cultures
- cultural and intercultural competence
- subject area competence
- professional and instrumental competence.
- attitudinal or psycho-physiological competence
- interpersonal competence
- strategic competence.

The individual competences included under each of these broad headings are very varied in nature: some of them consist of declarative knowledge or know-what, others more of skills, procedural knowledge or know-how, others more of attitudes. Whilst it is relatively simple to organize individual teaching modules around traditionally knowledge-based competences, that is not the case with skills-based and even less so with attitude-based competences. Traditionally, of course, courses have been almost exclusively declarative knowledge-driven and hence the issue of how to ensure learning and acquiring of skills and attitudinal competences, and how to organize them has not arisen. Recent research seems to indicate, furthermore, that compartmentalization has a negative effect on coordinated or networked learning. As we mentioned briefly in the previous chapter, the risk of students not establishing links between overly hermetic units and thus not developing overall translator competence should be taken into account at the organizational design stage. We will return to this point at the end of this chapter.

In order to examine possible models and their applicability to different contexts, we have chosen a series of case studies of course structures, the first of which we will analyse in depth in the next few pages. The remaining three have been provided as material for further analysis by readers.

Case study 1: the core content of the current Spanish undergraduate degree (Licenciatura) in Translating and Interpreting

The context
The Spanish university system is highly centralized, following the French tradition. Currently, this implies that there is a national "catalogue" of undergraduate degree courses which are recognized as valid; for each of these there is a centrally established core content (usually around 40%) which must be present in

all courses run by Spanish universities offering each particular degree. Individual course structures, based on this core content, require ministerial approval in order to run. The system is traditionally content (declarative knowledge)-based; there is currently no requirement for objectives to be made explicit, or for other kinds of competences to be developed by university courses. Some of these aspects are under reform, within the framework of the European Higher Education Area: future courses will be defined in terms of core competences, derived from objectives, and approaches are to become more student/learner-orientated, but the high level of centralization is not only unlikely to change, but is in fact likely to have a greater impact on university-level course design, as the Ministry is currently contemplating increasing core elements to up to 60% of each curriculum. This means that Spanish courses are and will continue to be remarkably homogeneous in nature; the fact that there are currently some 20 four- or five-year full undergraduate courses running in Translation, with an estimated 7000 students, makes this case study an interesting one.

The system is credit-based. Unlike other credit-based systems, however, the traditional Spanish credit is measured in **face-to-face** class contact time, and defined as 10 hours' teaching, with only limited potential to account for other activities (up to three hours per credit may be devoted to academically supervised activities, but in practice few universities actually authorize reduction of face-to-face class time). This means that the average 300-credit course, normally taught over four years, with few exceptions taking five, consists of 75 credits per year, and students are in face-to-face classroom teaching situations on average 25 hours per week! Reform underway within the European Higher Education Area implies a change in the definition of the credit, and a move from the extremely teacher-centred approach reflected in its current definition to a more student-centred approach. The credit will be redefined as on average 25 hours of student effort or input, covering face-to-face class time, learning activities of all kinds outside the classroom, tutorial attention and support, examinations, and so on. This should imply a considerable reduction in class time, possibly to around 15 hours a week, although some reform proposals circulating at the time of writing suggest that students may still have to be in formal classroom situations some 20 hours a week.

It is important to note that despite this system, many teachers have managed to design very innovative syllabuses; indeed a great deal of innovative work on translator training in recent years has been produced in Spain (see for example Hurtado 1999, or González Davies 2003 and 2004). Obviously, however, if the system is adapted to a more learner-centred approach, these innovations will be more easily implemented and incorporated into practice.

It is also pertinent to indicate as part of this contextualization that the only degrees offered at present in Spain relating to languages are traditional four-year Philology (language and literature) courses, three-year primary teacher-training diplomas for future primary teachers specializing in language teaching, a two-year second cycle degree in Linguistics, and this full four-year course in Translating and Interpreting. This situation means that the onus of non-traditional or applied language training in general has been tacitly (never explicitly) laid on the discipline of Translation, which inevitably has to deal with an enormous demand from students who do not necessarily want to become translators or interpreters, but rather are looking for training in professional applications of languages in general (in other countries Applied Languages and similar degrees). It will become clear that this factor was not taken into account in the design of the core curriculum; it is also the case that universities offering Translation degrees are loath to admit this apparent over-specialization.

Let us move on to examine the core curriculum itself. Remember that the credits listed here are the compulsory elements for all degrees in Translating and Interpreting. The number of credits in each area may be increased by individual universities, although universities are equally free only to offer these specific credits and fill in the rest of the curriculum with optional courses set up for other degree courses. This option, which is perceived – rightly or wrongly – as saving on resources, has actually been implemented by at least one Spanish university, and others have partially followed this trend by adding only very little translation-specific content to the core.

Core curriculum

1st cycle	
Documentary Research for Translation	4 credits (40 hours)
Language A (official institutional language/s)	8 credits (80 hours)
Language B (first foreign language, taken from an advanced level)	12 credits (120 hours)
Language C (second foreign language, taken ab initio in many cases)	12 credits (120 hours)
Linguistics Applied to Translation	6 credits (60 hours)
Theory and Practice of Translation	6 credits (60 hours)
2nd cycle	
Computing Applied to Translation	4 credits (40 hours)
Techniques for Consecutive Interpreting	8 credits (80 hours)
Techniques for Simultaneous Interpreting	8 credits (80 hours)
Terminology	8 credits (80 hours)
Specialized Translation	20 credits (200 hours)
General Translation C-A	10 credits (100 hours)

Total compulsory core elements 48 + 58 = 106 (35% of 300 credits)

Figure 8. Core curriculum for Translating and Interpreting degrees in Spain

The underlying assumptions of this structure are many and varied and have an inevitable impact on how translators are being trained today in Spain. A brief summary of these is listed here. (See Mayoral 2001b for alternative comment on this training model.)

Languages: it is assumed that students require two working languages other then their "mother tongue". Mayoral (forthcoming) comments that this is probably a leftover from the time when most professional translators trained to work in international organizations, where requirements were for at least two foreign languages. The languages are classified according to the AIIC **A-B-C** scale (whereby A is native language/s, B active acquired language/s, and C passive acquired language/s), but applied to the institution, not to individual students, thus giving rise to complex linguistic combinations for a growing body of both home and international students. In bilingual regions, such as Catalonia or the Basque Country, two A languages are offered, but nowhere has a foreign language been offered, despite, for example, the enormous demand from Arabic-speaking students in Spain for this kind of option. These students simply have to fit into the fiction that Spanish, or Catalan, Basque or Galician is their A language.

In the secondary school system, normally only one language is taught to any degree of proficiency, and the languages on offer are limited essentially to English and French; this means that C languages must be learnt ab initio, thus necessitating simultaneous acquisition of language and translation competence. This may also be said often to be the case of B languages, in which many students entering courses have only intermediate levels, particularly in those cases where languages other than English and French are offered as B.

Theoretical content: the core obliges all universities to include theoretical content in both Linguistics and Translation Studies at an early stage of training, with no obligation to return to theory later on in the course, after practical translation experience has been acquired. This implies a belief in a deductive approach, that is that learning begins with theory which is then applied to practice. Most educational research today would question this (see chapter 3), suggesting that inductive approaches are more efficient. Recent, and very welcome, reconciliation between Linguistics and Translation has meant that the original debate over whether or not Linguistics should be included has now all but disappeared.

Translating and/or Interpreting: probably the most controversial aspect of this core curriculum has been the joint nature of the degree, not only imposing at least basic training in Interpreting for all, but also calling the degree "Translating and Interpreting". This is felt to be excessive and unnecessary by practically the entire TI community in Spain, particularly because the two areas of Interpreting included in the core are highly specialized and do not coincide with what could be considered basic oral skills for professional translators.

General and specialized translation: distinction is made between general and specialized translation without further definition of what "general" means, or how specialized translation skills should be. The underlying assumption is that general translation is easier than specialized translation, a dubious assumption many professional translators would question, if by "general texts" or "general translation" we mean the translation of literary or media texts, for example. There is fairly extensive agreement that even highly specialized texts from fields such as medicine or engineering may be easier to translate than highly culture-bound, expressive texts, often referred to as "general". There is some consensus regarding the kinds of text best used in the initial stages of translator training (highly conventionalised or standardized, short, and meaningful to the learner, for example; see Chapter 7), and "general" is definitely not the best description that can be found for them. (See Hurtado 1996 for further comment.)

Instrumental competences: the core was highly innovative in its day in including instrumental skills at the time (1991) infrequent on translation courses in other countries, although today much more commonplace. Most specialists are in strong agreement with their presence; disagreement arises, however, with regard to how that presence should be organized and in which order. Computing is in the second cycle, for example, although computing skills are necessary for any modern documentary research process, which is in the first cycle. Documentary Research is separated from Terminology, despite the fact that much documentary research carried out by translators is essentially terminological in its purpose. In most universities, there is no link established among these three areas or between them and practical translation activities. This is particularly the case because academic organizational structures mean the course units are assigned to different departments, and there is little or no tradition of intra-, let alone inter-departmental coordination.

Directionality: The detail of the curriculum (not reproduced here due to lack of space, but available in the Spanish Official Gazette of 30th September 1991) establishes that translation between A and B languages must be bi-directional. It is not clear on which assumption this requirement is based: it may be tacit recognition of the need for translation into B languages on the professional market, although it is more likely to be a reflection of the belief that translating into a foreign language is a good way of improving language skills. Whatever the reason, all students are thus required to reach a certain level in A-B translation. In some universities, this is extended to C languages also (probably further indication that A-B/C translation has been included essentially as a language acquisition exercise, if we remember that C languages are learned from scratch, or if we return to the AIIC definition of C languages as purely passive in professional practice). The result, however, is that training is taking place in at least two translational directions, probably rendering it richer and more complete.

Case study 2: *European initiatives to harmonize Translation degrees*

Over the years there have been several initiatives at European level to harmonize courses in Translation at university level. Prior to the beginning of the Bologna process (leading to the European Higher Education Area), two of the most interesting of these were carried out by the European Language Council (ELC), a thematic network formed by a dozen or so universities offering translator and/or interpreter training courses, and by the European Centre of the International Federation of Translators (FIT). The latter is known as POSI (Praxis-orientierte Studieninhalte/practice-oriented study content for the training of translators), and as a FIT initiative involved a large number of European universities, professional bodies and FIT member associations. There have since been later initiatives, often at national level with international consultation within the framework of the Bologna university reform process. For our second case study, given its initial repercussion and the resources mobilized to produce it, we have taken the POSI study, and reproduce here one of its interim proposals for an overall course structure as described in an internal working document.

First Year – Methodology
Simultaneous teaching as appropriate of methodology of translation, theory of translation, intercultural metalinguistic knowledge, text analysis, editorial skill in the mother tongue, summaries of printed texts, terminology, search for background information and documentation, basic knowledge in informatics and language technology.

Second Year
Devoted mainly to translation exercises in numerous fields and a deepening of the cultural background in the different languages.
Practising translation of economic, legal, technical, medical, pharmaceutical and biological subject matters, enlisting the cooperation of representatives from other faculties, industry, EU experts and others.
Emphasis on speedy work while retaining highest possible quality. This entails switching attention from one subject to another while translating and work on translations in teams. Study of the history of translation.

Third Year – Internships
The third year should be divided into two different paid or unpaid six-month internships, each with industry and/or an international organization.
Guidelines for the trainee to be agreed upon between the University and the employer. Contact to be maintained via e-mail/Internet between the trainee and the University during the internship.

Fourth Year
Resumption of translation practice, branching out into psycholinguistics and neuro-sciences in addition to the subject matters studied in the second year. Preparation of thesis entailing both translation and original research.

Figure 9. Course structure proposal from the POSI project

Analyse this proposal from the following points of view:
- What would you say is the overall objective of this training programme?
- What are the general underlying assumptions made regarding translation? Regarding the role of the university? Regarding links with other training institutions and industry?
- How does this model deal with the dichotomy Translating/ Interpreting?
- What is assumed about students' language proficiency on entering?
- What does the model tell us about the local translation/interpretng market?
- What does the model tell us about the role of theory in translator training?
- What does the model tell us about directionality in translator training?
- In the first case study, we commented on the distinction between "general" and specialized translation. What approach does this proposal adopt to this issue?
- In what way does this proposal deal with instrumental competences?
- How is progression dealt with in this proposal? Is this approach appropriate in your opinion?
- Should trainee translators have to produce a thesis or dissertation at undergraduate level? And at postgraduate level? Should it entail both translation and original research? Why (in order to attain which learning outcomes)?
- Would this proposal be viable at your institution or in your context? Comment on the elements which may make it hard to implement.
- Comment on any other points of interest you find in the proposal.

Case study 3*: Masters of Arts in Translation and Interpreting at Macquarie University, Sydney, Australia*

This is an Australian postgraduate course "designed to meet the needs of those who have good linguistic skills and are seeking to develop professionally as translators or interpreters and to acquire a higher degree. The program is offered in a number of languages depending on demand and resources. Chinese, Japanese, Korean, Spanish and Thai are currently available and French may be offered if the level of interest is high enough. Apart from professional training, the course includes theory of translation and a research component". The course lasts 18 months if taken full-time and two to three years if taken part-time.

It consists of the following core units: Theory and Practice in Translation; Introduction to Text Analysis; Interpreting Techniques; Research Methods in Translation and Interpreting; Public Speaking, Advanced Writing Skills for Translators and Cross-Cultural Pragmatics.

And the following elective units: Computing in Translation; Translation Practice; Interpreting Practice; Language Transfer in the Media; Lexicography; Community Interpreting and Translating; Dissertation; Advanced Translation; Grammar, Meaning and Discourse; Languages and Cultures in Contact; Stylistics and Translation of Literature; Managing Cultural Diversity in Business; Managerial Marketing; The International System; Theory of International Relations and International Political Economy.

(Information available at: http://www.ling.mq.edu.au/postgraduate/coursework/tip/mati.htm)

Figure 10. Course structure of the MA in Translating and Interpreting at Macquarie University, Sydney, Australia

Consult the programme in more detail at the official website and then analyse this postgraduate course by answering the questions given for Case Study 2 above.

Case Study 4: *Screen Translation Studies MA Leeds University, UK*

This is a 12-month (24-month part-time) postgraduate course which "addresses the growing demands of the visual media market for highly qualified

linguists capable of creating mono- and inter-lingual subtitles. It familiar-
ises students with the linguistic, cultural and technical constraints on screen
translating, dubbing and subtitling and with the various techniques for over-
coming them."

"In a phased introduction to general and then more subject-specific skills,
all students follow the core modules on methods and approaches (semester
1) and specialised translation (semesters 1 and 2) shared with the two other
MA courses. All students also take the specialised modules on text com-
pression and monolingual subtitling (semester 1), audio-visual text analysis
and film translation and subtitling (semester 2). Additionally, students choose
from a variety of optional modules offered by the Centre for Translation
Studies and the School of Modern Languages and Cultures. A summer
project will address practical or theoretical issues of screen translation."

The list of optional modules at the time of writing is: Specialised Translation (from a second language); Investigating Translation; Machine
Translation; Technical Communication for Translators; Stylistics; Seman-
tics; Discourse Analysis.

(Information available at: http://www.smlc.leeds.ac.uk/cts/cts_content/
ma_programmes/masts.asp)

*Figure 11. Course structure of the MA in Screen Translation
at Leeds University, United Kingdom*

Consult the programme in more detail at the official website and then
analyse this specialist postgraduate course by answering the questions
given for Case Study 2 above.

If you prefer, of course, you may apply this set of questions and further
analysis to any other translator training programme including , especially,
your own.

Some general considerations on course content and its organization

After these case studies, which will hopefully have given you food for thought,
let us turn to some general considerations on translator training course content.
Alongside our repeated concern for each course to be designed in its own context, taking into account its own constraints and environment, we do also believe

that there are common elements to many if not all training situations, to which we will now devote some time. The following are some general considerations on areas of competence and other issues in relation to overall course design and planning. Chapter 6 will expand on ideas for specific teaching and learning activities designed to facilitate the acquisition of competences; chapter 7 will deal in detail with progression and sequencing.

> These comments are general reflections on course organization and planning, some of which will be more applicable to your context than others. As you read them, for each section, note down what the current situation is in your context. How do the comments I make apply to your course? In what way?

Language competence

Effective course design must bear in mind the real level of language competence of potential and actual students. This is true of all languages involved in the training process, including "A" or "native" languages. This may mean that in some contexts, translation simply cannot begin to be learned in the early stages of training courses. This should be recognized explicitly, and language classes should not be disguised as translation classes.

Where languages are taught on translation programmes, close coordination between staff is essential. Language teaching could centre on the particular language skills a translator requires: textual knowledge rather than theoretical knowledge of the phonetic system, for example, although the differentiation runs the risk of becoming artificial.

It is also very positive if programmes take into account the real language combination of each student, avoiding fictitious situations such as those referred to above where native-speakers of foreign languages must take courses as if they were native speakers of the institution's official language(s). This may be difficult at times, but is probably the only way to ensure some degree of effectiveness in learning and of fairness in assessment. Clearly this cannot mean that every institution has to offer every possible language combination on all its translation courses, rather simply that teaching and administrative staff and structures should recognize real individual situations. Native English-speaking students with German and Russian B languages, for example, would be able to register at German-speaking institutions as English A, German and Russian B, and take German-Russian translation courses, without their academic record reflecting fictitious native proficiency in either Russian or German. That is, this combination is B-B for them, never A-B nor B-A. Many students, particularly of less widely spoken languages, have to train to become translators in this kind of linguistic environment, transferring the skills acquired to translation practice into and out of their real A languages. It would also be positive if institutions were to offer advanced level courses for non-native speakers of the official language of the institution in order to facilitate learning for these students, who will become more and more the rule as student mobility and the internationalization of higher education grow.

Cultural competence

Traditionally, translator training programmes have included courses on what is known as "Civilization" or "Area Studies" in order to ensure trainees learn about the "cultures" of their working languages. While recognizing the usefulness of much of this kind of encyclopaedic knowledge, it is true that much of it is today available easily for anyone with basic research skills. Moreover, culture is a much broader concept than simple institutional, historical and geographical knowledge about different peoples and societies. For translators, it is essential to acquire competence (know-how) in their working cultures' perceptions, myths, beliefs, values, stereotypes, and so on. (See Katan, 1999/2003 for an excellent, thorough-going monograph on the subject.) It is likely that alongside traditional learning about cultures, translator trainees should acquire cultural and intercultural competence by immersion in other cultures, through – for example – mobility programmes, exchanges and contact with students from other cultures at their own home institutions. It is, fortunately, increasingly common and easy to incorporate mobility (whether real or virtual) into training programmes, and full advantage should be taken of these opportunities. The more integrated these activities are into course design, the more effective learning will be through them.

A final point to be made here is that cultural competence for translators can only begin with knowledge of their own culture, arising from a certain distancing from it, which is practically impossible without direct contact (with or without mobility) with other cultures.

Instrumental competence

The essential aspect of instrumental competences on training programmes is for them to be understood as such: as instruments applicable to the end which is acquiring translator competence.

It is obvious that professional translators must be familiar with translation technologies, how to use them, and also be able to appraise how they affect the translation process. The following is a very brief summary of an interesting and well-reasoned classification of six areas which trainee translators should cover in this area, proposed by Alcina (forthcoming):

* The translator's computer

- Communication and documentary research
- Word-processing and desk-top publishing.
- Linguistic tools and resources
- Translation tools
- Localization tools

An issue to be dealt with here by training institutions and trainers is the choice of computer applications to include in the syllabus. There is considerable pressure to use the most widely accepted and best known translation memory software, for example, despite the enormous expense that this entails for institutions. It is probably more appropriate on training programmes to help students to learn and understand the basics of translation memory technology in general, without necessarily learning any one particular commercial programme. The same holds for subtitling software and other similar applications. Fortunately, commercial programmes work on essentially the same principles and are becoming increasingly compatible, thus allowing educational institutions to work with freeware, but at the same time allowing students to develop basic skills which can then be transferred to any commercial package.

Professionalization

Professionalization on translator training courses can take a variety of forms, depending of the overall degree of professionalization aimed at on the programme, orthe level students are at, among other factors. Simulation of professional practice (through realistic translation briefs, deadlines and other submission requirements, for example) is fairly standard on translation courses today. Explicit relating of teaching and learning activities to professional environments is also common ("We are doing this exercise because professional translators are often required to xxx"). Role-play, with students assuming different roles for different tasks (client, reviser, terminologist, layout specialist, as well as translator) is also a fairly widespread technique. Some courses even incorporate highly technical, although also strongly environment-bound, abilities such as producing an invoice into class activity. It is important for these activities to be carefully contextualized, as rote learning of how to carry them out may be counterproductive in a professional environment (tax laws vary not only from country to country, but even within countries and also over time).

Alongside these, opportunities may be offered for students to see how translation service providers work *in situ* by visiting agencies or organizations, or receiving visits from professionals (often graduates from their own course, which is in itself motivating). And last but certainly not least, work placements have increasingly become part of training programmes. See Chapter 5 on resources for more detailed discussion of this point.

As we saw in Chapter 1, some authors (Kiraly, Gouadec, Vienne) advocate the carrying out of real, not simulated translation commissions in class, with students actually taking on responsibility for a real professional task under the guidance of the teacher, and charging the client for the work done. This kind of activity, at the right (final) stage of training and with good supervision is certainly very enriching for trainees, although it does pose certain problems in relation with the profession (some would regard this kind of activity as unfair competition), and does require the client to be aware of the circumstances in which his/her translation will be carried out (with all the concomitant implications for deadlines, quality, confidentiality, and so on). It may, furthermore, also be difficult to fit into rigid academic timetabling, not to mention accounting practices! What happens if the right commission does not crop up at the beginning of the course, for example? These contingencies must also be written into course design.

Interpersonal competence

Translation is increasingly a team activity. The longstanding stereotype of the lonely translator sitting at home surrounded by books is nowadays quite unrepresentative of most translators' professional environments. Academic settings often tend, however, through activities and assessment practices, to promote an individual work ethic, or even competition among students. Introducing team work and collective responsibility (for assessment for example) will help recent graduates in the transition to the world of work; it will also develop a much-demanded generic competence. It is important for course designers and teachers to be aware that the ability to work in a team is not developed simply by organizing students into workgroups, but rather that specific skills need to be acquired consciously through practice and reflection. For further detail, see chapter 6, on teaching and learning activities.

Subject area competence

The issue of subject area competence for the translator has been the subject of much debate, and lies at the root of many assumptions made professionally. The European Union employs graduates in Law to work as legal translators, for example. Job advertisements looking for graduates in Medicine to carry out medical translation tasks have not disappeared from the press. The underlying assumption is that subject area knowledge is more important than translator competence. This is hotly disputed by most translation specialists, who do recognise, however, that the more subject area knowledge a professional translator has, the better for the practice of specialized translation. The problem faced by most undergraduate training courses is that it is practically impossible to offer training in a specialized field and in translation at the same time and within the time confines of a standard degree. At postgraduate level, this problem is much more easily addressed. A further constraint is the risk of overspecialisation, and subsequent limiting of job opportunities. It is important for each course to study this issue in depth for its own context, to establish policy in this regard and to make this policy explicit for all stakeholders (authorities, teaching staff, students).

Most general undergraduate training courses offer introductory modules to broad subject areas such as economics, law, medicine, computer technology, engineering (often as optional modules either within their own programme structure or in other faculties or departments), with the aim of students acquiring sufficient basic knowledge to understand the major concepts in specialized texts, and to carry out in-depth documentary research for translation in a meaningful way. Experience normally indicates that the more specifically designed these courses are for translators, and the greater the comprehension of the translation process teaching staff have, the more successful they are for the acquisition of translation-relevant skills.

Attitudinal competence

It has until now been infrequent to find attitudinal elements, at least explicitly, in course design. The more student-centred higher education becomes, and the more generic skills come to be recognized as important social competences, the more attitudinal elements are being incorporated into training programmes. In TS literature, it is not infrequent to find references to student self-concept, confidence, awareness. For authors such as Kiraly (2000), this is a key element of translator education. As with other areas of competence, socialization as a professional translator is not something which occurs automatically on all training courses. There is no doubt that courses reproducing professional environments, and promoting active student responsibility in translation situations will be more successful in facilitating the development of attitudinal competences, than those organized in more traditional academic ways, with mostly passive student involvement.

Unitization/networking

Traditionally, university programmes are organized in small component parts, which we have been calling modules. As we have seen above, for example, translation programmes will often include modules on information technology for translators, on terminology and documentary research, or on various kinds of specialized translation, which kinds usually depending on the context. Students will normally be required to take certain core modules and offered a choice from a range of optional modules. Such a structure can afford a particular programme considerable flexibility, and of course allows for the subdivision of the overall competences to be acquired into smaller more manageable, more easily assessable units. The danger of this compartmentalization is, however, that from the students' point of view it can be difficult to establish relations between the different component parts. A first year "Documentary Research Skills" module, once taken and passed, is rarely associated with a second year "Introduction to Professional Translation" module, although the competences acquired on the former should in fact be an essential element for learning on the latter. Calvo (2001), researching the step from initial translator training to more specialized modules at advanced level finds that students fail to establish links between the various elements making up their course, thus preventing them from perceiving an overall picture of translation and their learning process. The internal politics of academic institutions, misled conceptions of academic freedom, and a lack of institutional mechanisms to promote coordination are identified as some of the factors leading to this de-structuring of learning.

It is the case that the rigid application of the list of competences and, perhaps more so, their assignation to particular departments at universities with inflexible bureaucratic systems have given rise to a sadly impermeable set of separate compartments of knowledge which are rarely approached from the co-ordinated networking perspective which is so necessary for full development of translation competence. This failure does underline the need for rethinking aspects of some training programmes.

In this vein, there are clearly areas of competence in the list above that would never constitute individual modules on a training programme, so generic or cross-curricular are they in nature. It is difficult, for example, to imagine a module in "Strategies and organization". These areas necessarily give rise to cross-curricular learning outcomes shared by many if not all modules. Indeed, it is these less content- and more process-oriented competences which may lead to the design of curricula for more truly "aligned" or coordinated learning. Much internal coordination is needed in the writing of specific learning outcomes for individual modules; explicit agreement is needed in the sequencing of learning, and flexible solutions are required for the organization of advanced modules, where prior learning of individual competences should come together to form overall translator competence (definable in this case perhaps in something akin to Pym's terms – see Chapter 2 above – as an ability to generate a target text series and informedly to choose one appropriate solution for each translation situation).

This chapter has offered a framework for reflection on overall course design, in two ways. Firstly, case studies allow analysis of different solutions to course design, which you will have related to your own context. Secondly, some of the major issues involved are analysed individually at a general level. Your reflection on how each of these relates to your own context will provide a useful background to work in later chapters.

Further reading

Alcina, Amparo (forthcoming) 'Translation Technologies: A Description of the Field and the Classification of Tools and Resources'. *Perspectives.*

Full core content for the current Spanish undergraduate (*licenciatura*) course in Translating and Interpreting is to be found in the Spanish Official Gazette, *Boletín Oficial del Estado*, 30-09-1991.

Gabr, Moustafa (2001) 'Toward a Model Approach to Translation Curriculum Development'. *Translation Journal*, Volume 5 N° 2, available at: http://www.accurapid.com/journal/16edu.htm

Li, Defeng (2000) 'Needs Assessment in Translation Teaching: Making Translator Training More Responsive to Social Needs'. *Babel*, 46:4. 289-299.

Mayoral (2001) 'Por una renovación en la formación de traductores e intérpretes: revisión de algunos de los conceptos sobre los que se basa el actual sistema, su estructura y contenidos'. *Sendebar* n° 12. 311-336.

5. Resources, Old and New

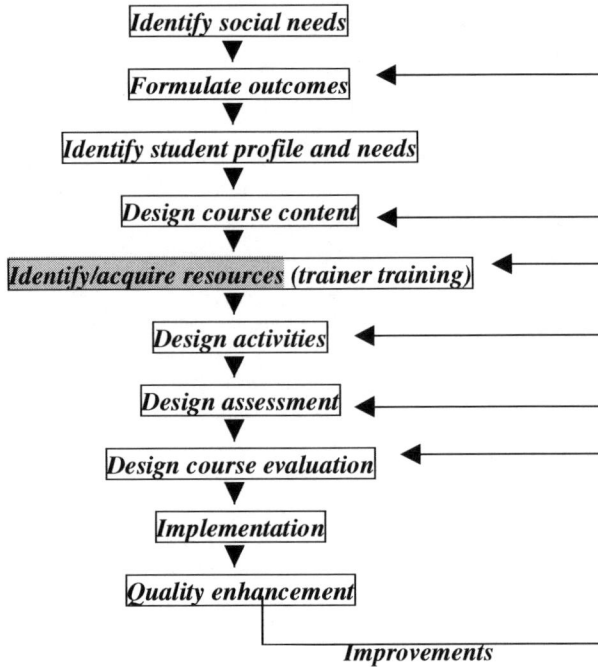

```
                    ┌─────────────────────┐
                    │Identify social needs│
                    └─────────────────────┘
                               ▼
                    ┌──────────────────┐
                    │Formulate outcomes│◄──────────────────────────┐
                    └──────────────────┘                           │
                               ▼                                   │
            ┌───────────────────────────────┐                      │
            │Identify student profile and needs│                   │
            └───────────────────────────────┘                      │
                               ▼                                   │
                ┌────────────────────┐                             │
                │Design course content│◄──────────────────────┐   │
                └────────────────────┘                         │   │
                               ▼                               │   │
        ┌────────────────────────────────────────┐            │   │
        │Identify/acquire resources (trainer training)│◄───────┼─┐ │
        └────────────────────────────────────────┘            │ │ │
                               ▼                               │ │ │
                    ┌────────────────┐                         │ │ │
                    │Design activities│◄───────────────────────┘ │ │
                    └────────────────┘                           │ │
                               ▼                                 │ │
                    ┌─────────────────┐                          │ │
                    │Design assessment│◄─────────────────────────┘ │
                    └─────────────────┘                            │
                               ▼                                   │
                ┌──────────────────────┐                           │
                │Design course evaluation│◄─────────────────────────┘
                └──────────────────────┘
                               ▼
                    ┌──────────────┐
                    │Implementation│
                    └──────────────┘
                               ▼
                    ┌───────────────────┐
                    │Quality enhancement│
                    └───────────────────┘
                               └──────────────────────────────┐
                                 Improvements
```

Summary and aims

In this chapter, the central theme is that of resources, and their role in
training programmes. The concept of resources will be taken in the broadest possible sense and, as the title suggests, will cover both traditional
and less traditional resources normally at the disposal of translator trainers. By the end of the chapter, you should be aware of a wide range of
potential resources for training, be able to identify those most easily us-
able in your context, and be able to evaluate their usefulness for specific
purposes. The following will be understood to constitute resources for
translator training: physical environment (classrooms, computer rooms,
study rooms, library, office environment); traditional resources (textbooks,
texts, blackboard, whiteboard, overhead projectors and so on); new technologies (computer-based learning resources in general); mobility
programmes and related resources (staff and student exchanges and cooperative projects); work placements and related resources (outside
experts; professionals, visits; cooperative projects).

Physical environment

Classroom organization tells us a great deal about dominant teaching styles and attitudes to teaching and learning within an institution. Traditional classroom arrangements typically have students sitting passively in rows, all looking towards the teacher, who has a central place, often even on an elevated platform, at which to stand (or sit) and from which to talk to the listening class. This physical organization implies a strongly transmissionist and teacher-centred approach to teaching and learning. Students are not encouraged to look at or talk to each other, it is difficult to move around the classroom, so that even teachers wanting to break with traditional methods have serious difficulty in doing so. Often the furniture itself is not suitable for practical activities such as consulting several dictionaries at once in a small group and noting down possible solutions, as it has been designed simply for students to take lecture notes. More participative classrooms will allow different organizations of the furniture for different activities. For whole group activities, a circle or U-shaped distribution is often recommended, as this allows all participants to see each other and be seen, encouraging participation. For other activities, students should be able to sit comfortably in groups or in pairs; students should have large desks or tables (or be able to construct these by joining small desks together), on which to place dictionaries, laptops or other resources, and around which to organize group discussions; teachers should be able to move around, talking to small groups or individual students. Institutions keen on spending large amounts on money on installing expensive IT equipment are often unfortunately loath to spend money on simple things like new movable furniture for classrooms.

Curiously, the same problem occurs with seemingly modern computer room facilities. Despite their modern appearance, these often reproduce at least partially the traditional distribution of a classroom, with students in rows from which they can see the teacher (often with difficulty because the computer gets in the way!), but not all the other students in the class. Attempts to fit as many computers as possible into small spaces often lead to overly narrow corridor spaces between rows of computers, where the teacher and students cannot move around, and students cannot sit together in groups at monitors for team work. The equipment itself often makes whole-group or plenary presentations difficult to see and thus to follow.

If we are to use participative teaching and learning activities, it is imperative that we have an appropriate physical space in which to do so, whether by design of the institution or by making ad hoc individual changes to classroom arrangements where possible.

Think of the classrooms you are going to work in. How is the furniture distributed? Where and how do the students sit? Where is the teacher's space situated? Is the furniture appropriate for the activities you want to carry out? Can the students sit together in groups? Can you (and they) move around from group to group or individual to individual? Are there ways you can modify the classroom arrangement to make it more condu- cive to the activities you plan to carry out?

Similar considerations can be made regarding student facilities for independ- ent work and study. As the emphasis moves from teaching to learning, it becomes increasingly necessary for institutions to provide resources and spaces for stu- dents to work autonomously. This is especially important for translator training programmes, as students will normally be required to do a considerable amount of translation and other work outside the classroom itself. Traditional libraries, where silence is the golden rule, will not constitute appropriate work space for students working collaboratively in groups and thus needing to talk. Institutions should provide spacious rooms with large working surfaces, movable chairs and tables, and computer facilities with Internet connections where students can carry out translations and related tasks outside the classroom.

Alongside these facilities, resources for documentary research should be available to students, both in the form of a well-stocked traditional library, and in the form of free and permanent Internet access.

What independent study rooms are available to students at your institu- tion? Are they suitable for the activities you have planned for your students outside the classroom? If not, can any measures be taken to remedy this? Can you modify the activities to adapt to the resources available?

Are all the resources you plan to ask students to use available at your institution? In particular, are all the dictionaries and other class resources you will recommend in your syllabus available at the library, or on an Intranet or the Internet? Is access to the Intranet and/or the Internet freely available to all students?

A final word on physical space, this time for tutorial support activities for students. Student-centred learning requires strong student support, and hence physical spaces which enable individual and small group sessions between teach- ers and students. This kind of tutorial work is often carried out in staff offices, which are not always entirely suitable. They may be too small to attend groups of four or five students; they may be shared with other members of staff, thus preventing any degree of privacy; they may not be appropriately furnished. Again, institutions should be pressed to offer suitable provision for this essential part of teaching and learning activities.

> Where will you be carrying out your support and follow-up work with students? Is it a suitable place? Does it allow you to ensure confidentiality?

Traditional classroom resources

The most traditional classroom resource is probably the blackboard, or alternatives such as the whiteboard or flipchart. The basic principle behind the use of the blackboard is also applicable to resources such as the overhead projector (OHP) and PowerPoint or similar computer-based presentation tools. They all constitute visual support for information otherwise offered only orally in a lecture situation. Research shows that information which is received multi-sensorially is processed more easily (Biggs 2003: 80; Robinson 2003: 248-249), and so accompanying a presentation or a lecture with (at least) visual support facilitates understanding and hence learning (see also chapter 6 for detail on teaching and learning activities). In the case of translation, these resources are even more useful for class activities as they permit whole group presentations of source texts, draft translations, alternative texts in written form for classroom analysis. As translation deals with written text, this is particularly important. The hopefully now infrequent traditional custom of reading aloud fragments of draft translation in class for discussion prevents us from analysing many essential aspects of written text: textual cohesion cannot be analysed in short oral fragments; formal aspects such as punctuation, spelling, typography or layout cannot be analysed in oral form; written texts simply do not work in the same way as texts intended to be read aloud; finally, when a text is read aloud fragment by fragment, students are forced to devote considerable effort to using their short-term memory, thus occupying cognitive resources they could be using to analyse and discuss translation problems and solutions. Resources for visual presentation of written text are thus essential in any translation classroom.

The basic rules for the use of all kinds of visual support are the same, whether they be blackboard, OHP or PowerPoint:

- when giving information, do not give too much at once;
- write clearly and/or use large enough font size to allow easy reading;
- do not talk to the blackboard or to the computer: address those listening;
- do not turn your back on the audience or look down and/or aside for long periods of time to write on the board, the OHP slide, or to look at the computer screen.

These simple basic recommendations can also be offered to students making presentations or offering translations or other texts for class discussion. This will help them to develop the very useful generic competence of speaking in public, a much demanded skill which many people find extremely hard to master. Clearly, computer-based presentation programmes such as PowerPoint facilitate the task at hand, avoiding problems such as hand-writing which is hard to read, insufficient space on the blackboard, wasting class time writing long texts on the board, the need for masking (partially covering an OHP slide to gradually reveal the points being made), and so on. But simply putting everything we or our students want to say in class on slides for the computer does not necessarily make for a good presentation. The basics of public speaking, presentations and lectures are the same whatever the media we use as visual support. (See further reading.)

Which visual support media are available in the rooms you will usually be teaching in? Which do you intend to use for your classes? For which activities? Will the students also be using them?

Prepare a brief set of instructions for students using these media in class to enhance their presentation techniques.

The second basic traditional teaching resource is the textbook. There exist quite a number of textbooks to be used as such on translation courses, but it probably true to say that most translator trainers prefer to develop their own material. There are several reasons for this. Firstly, many text types have a short shelf-life, and thus textbooks rapidly go out of date. Secondly, as we have insisted throughout this book, translator training courses must be designed for their local context, thus making textbooks offering material for many different situations unlikely to be successful. Thirdly, many translator trainers who are also professional translators prefer to use in class material they have already translated professionally, thus taking full advantage of their professional experience. Fourthly, many of the textbooks available seem to have been designed for language learning approaches to translation, rather than for fully fledged professional training courses. Textbooks in the traditional sense of a course-book to be followed from beginning to end as the basis for a module are, therefore, in fact a little-used resource in translator training. This does not of course mean that no appropriate textbooks are available on the market, nor that existing textbooks do not offer useful suggestions for activities which you can adapt to your particular module and context. Note that in this series, the approach adopted has been that of offering useful resources to teachers for them to adapt to their teaching situation; in particular the books do not usually include actual texts for translation.

> Are you aware of the textbooks available for the particular course or module you are going to teach? Carry out a bibliographical search in order to identify those which may be of use. Are they recent? Check in the index to see in what way they might be of use to you on your module. In which respects do you find they are suitable or otherwise for use on your module?

This means of course, that trainers spend much time searching for suitable class material, designing and preparing activities. Texts themselves, rather than textbooks, thus become essential resources for training. Criticism of traditional translator training has often centred on the kind of texts used, and the lack of appropriate criteria for text selection and activity design in general. This issue will be dealt with in depth in chapter 6 on teaching and learning activities and chapter 7, on sequencing. At this point, suffice it to say that trainers must have explicit and clear criteria for selecting and designing class activities and material, including texts for translation, and that these can normally be derived, in an aligned curricular design, from the intended learning outcomes for the unit or module in question.

New technologies

In teaching and learning, as in so many other aspects of life at the beginning of the XXIst century, new technologies have an essential role to play, and can facilitate many of the tasks involved. There is however a risk of associating pedagogical innovation with the medium itself, an approach adopted by many institutions as witnessed in their mission or policy statements. At my own institution, for example, innovative teaching practice is directly associated with the use of technology. Yet, simply using new technologies does not make teaching and learning either innovative or more effective. Biggs (2003: 214) points out that using information technology for teaching may even heighten the risk of returning to or maintaining purely transmissionist approaches. Putting lecture notes on an Intranet may seem innovative, but does not in fact enhance learning in any way; it simply facilitates access to information. The author prefers to use the term *education technology* in an attempt to remind teachers that the overall aim should be to enhance learning, not simply to give more information.

In translator training, the issue of new technologies is of course not only a question of using new technologies for teaching and learning, but also of helping students to learn how to use new technologies as applied to translation. That is a separate issue, dealt with briefly in chapter 4, under the heading "instrumental competence". In this chapter we will concentrate on the role of education technology as a training resource.

In what way can new technologies become education technologies? Biggs (2003) identifies four main areas: managing learning; engaging learners in appropriate learning activity; assessing learning; and distance or off-campus teaching. Let us examine each of these briefly in turn as they may be applied to translator training.

New technologies can prove to be of enormous help to teachers and trainers in managing teaching and learning activities in general. Web technology and email clearly facilitate tasks such as record keeping, lists and providing information for students. Probably more importantly, they facilitate communication between teachers and students, among teachers and among students. A common complaint among teaching staff is that email communication has increased their workload, as students now find it easier to ask more questions, make more direct requests, and also expect immediate replies. The up-side of this is that greater and easier communication between students and teachers is undoubtedly a good thing for better learning. The down-side is that, in effect, authorities often interpret new technologies as a cheap way of dealing with larger groups, and neglect to take into account the very real extent to which staff time is being taken up by their use. Because of this, it is probably necessary for staff to develop mechanisms for dealing with this new workload. Examples of these may be:

- pre-prepared replies to frequent questions (which can also be included on the module website or electronic bulletin board as FAQs);
- encourage peer consultation through email groups and forums;
- establishing a particular period of time each day for dealing with email relating to each module;
- explaining email etiquette to students (use of re line to indicate module and subject matter clearly, short concise messages, reading all relevant material on paper or on the website before writing with a question, as the answer is often already available, waiting a reasonable period of time for a reply, and so on).

Have you had any experience in communicating with students by email? In what way have you found email to be a useful means of communication with students? Have you identified any problems? In which ways could you make your use of email for communication with students more efficient?

Write brief instructions for the students on a particular module you teach on how to use email to communicate with you.

As to the second application, engaging learners in appropriate learning activity, there is no doubt that thoughtful use of education technology will allow this. New technologies make it easier, for example, to maintain constant contact with a whole class group, and within that class group, thus encouraging inter-student interaction; this is extremely easily achieved with email groups. These can simulate professional discussion groups (see Robinson 2003: 132 and Colina 2003: 55-60), promote debate, facilitate the provision of material prior to actual class sessions both by staff and by students; these usually **asynchronous** activities (not necessarily simultaneous for all involved) can be complemented with **synchronous** (simultaneous for all involved) activities such as chats or videoconferencing, allowing for example, the participation of external specialists in class activities, and student interaction with them. Note that recorded videoconferences can later be used as asynchronous activities.

On many occasions the application of new technologies to learning has been interpreted as replacing the traditional classroom with the computer lab as the site for class sessions. Where the facilities are available, this is an interesting option and is in general popular with students. There are also interesting commercial packages available allowing teacher monitoring and intervention in individual or group use of the computer by students, similar to those used previously in language laboratories. Teaching in computer labs allows the use of specific applications for specific tasks (depending, of course, on the software available), the simulation of a professional workstation (again when the appropriate software is available), and in particular means that help from the teacher is at hand to deal with practical problems, which is not necessarily the case when students use their own computers at home. It is important, however, to remember that the computer lab is a resource, not a teaching method as such and that the teacher will still have to write intended outcomes, analyse student profile, design appropriate learning activities and assess the actual outcomes in an aligned fashion. Alternatives to moving the entire class to the computer lab are using laptops and wireless connections in ordinary classrooms, either for individual and group work by students or for demonstrations of particular tasks.

> What facilities are available at your institution for the use of new technologies in teaching and learning activities? How do you intend to incorporate the use of new technologies into your teaching? In what way do you envisage engaging learners in appropriate activities through the use of new technologies? Will they be used in the classroom itself, or outside the classroom? Will their use be synchronous or asynchronous? Will their use be individual or collective?

Electronic assessment or computer-assisted assessment is normally most easily applied where assessment takes the form of multiple choice questions, and thus has perhaps less application to translator training than other aspects of education technology. It is of course possible to think of particular learning outcomes which can be measured and assessed in this way within translator training programmes, but they are few and far between. Education technology probably represents a step forward in the assessment of translation simply because it facilitates the submission or delivery of student translations by the same means as used professionally (email, ftp) and because word-processing software functions such as comment and change-tracing allow feedback from other students and teachers to be made easily also in electronic format.

> Could computer-assisted assessment be used on your module? If so, to assess which particular outcomes? Describe briefly how the assessment would be designed and implemented.

Finally, an obvious application of education technology is that of **distance or off-campus teaching and learning**. While this is a tremendous advance in that it allows the incorporation into higher education of students unable to travel to attend classes, and may facilitate higher education provision across frontiers, it is also true that institutions must be careful to measure their capability to offer sufficient and quality support and feedback to all those registered. Distance learning cannot simply be a way to offer training to enormous numbers of students at minimal cost. Quality provision requires extensive feedback, is time-consuming and hence necessitates quite intensive staffing, however distant those teachers may be from students. In translation, distance activities need not necessarily cover the entire curriculum, but do open up interesting opportunities for students temporarily away from university on exchange programmes, or on work placements, for example. Similarly, there is plenty of room for international cooperation in **tandem** and group work. Tandem work involves students from two institutions, often in two different countries with two different native languages, working together on translation or other tasks. Group work may take similar forms, except that more students are involved, allowing even more mixed language and nationality groups. An interesting example of this kind of international cooperation in translation is the Tradutech project coordinated by the Université de Rennes. (http://www.tradutech.net).

> Will you have any distance students on your module? How do you plan to use new technologies to facilitate learning for them?
>
> Can you think of activities for which distance tandem or group work would be appropriate? Which? For what reason, and with which aim in

mind? Do you have international partners with whom to carry out the activity? If not, how can you find partners for this kind of activity?

Mobility programmes

Earlier in this book, the internationalization of higher education was identified as one of the major trends affecting tertiary teaching and learning today. This is partly the cause and partly the result of the success of a number of student and staff mobility programmes, which have now become a standard integral part of university life. In this chapter, they will be dealt with as a learning resource for translator training programmes.

There is no doubt that an extended stay in another country is an important learning experience for any future graduate, which in the field of translation becomes practically essential. The historical forerunner of the student exchange is the Grand Tour, embarked upon by young aristocrats to acquire first-hand experience and knowledge of the cultural wonders usually of continental Europe, as well as a wealth of personal experiences intended to develop their personal maturity. Many years later, this originally elitist practice evolved into an integral part of undergraduate language courses in some countries, notably the United Kingdom and Ireland, with students taking a compulsory year abroad in countries where the language or languages studied were spoken. In the United States, normally highly structured year abroad programmes in Europe and in Asia also became popular, not only within languages departments, but as a general learning experience for students on any undergraduate or postgraduate programme. In many countries, financial constraints limited the extent to which these programmes were made available and taken up by students, also inhibited by fear of "wasting" a year where credit was not fully transferred. These problems were precisely those addressed by institutional programmes to promote mobility, especially from the eighties on.

Without a doubt the largest and most successful student mobility programme has been the Socrates-Erasmus programme launched by the then European Community in 1987. This programme, open to all disciplines, was designed to promote young Europeans' knowledge of other European countries and languages, and thus in the longer term to promote greater professional mobility and a sense of European identity. Over two million students have now participated in the programme since its inception seventeen years ago, and it has now become the seed for the European Higher Education Area, which intends to produce greater harmonization of European tertiary education and strengthen the role of Europe in global higher education provision. Apart from Socrates in Europe, students in universities the world over are offered opportunities to study on mobility programmes of many different kinds and promoted by many and varied governmental and non-governmental organizations. Many universities also run bilateral exchange programmes with institutions in other countries.

This kind of opportunity is a valuable learning resource and should be understood as such, that is, should be fully integrated into training programmes. For future translators the added value of a period of study abroad is evident. Briefly, the most obvious plus is in improved language competence and is particularly noticeable in oral skills, although there is no doubt that written skills also improve considerably. The second, and possibly more important, advantage is the development of cultural and intercultural competence. There is simply no better way to develop understanding of how another culture works than full immersion in the culture for an extended period of time at an appropriate stage of learning (see Chapter 13 in Katan 2003 for more detail on a developmental model of cultural competence). An important and often forgotten offshoot is also much heightened awareness and thus understanding of the student's native culture. It is difficult to understand the values of one's own culture until one is confronted with another culture's different values. Negotiating this difference constitutes important experiential learning of intercultural mediation. A third advantage is the opportunity to experience different learning and teaching styles, along with the opportunity to study areas not offered at home institutions. The personal development this kind of complex and impacting experience entails is another plus for the learner, who normally develops attitudinal competences such as self-confidence, organizational ability, self-awareness and so on. These generic skills are all directly applicable to translation activity.

Periods abroad have also been shown to have a positive impact on graduates' ability to find employment, and on graduates' readiness to take up work abroad (see for example Teichler and Jahr, 2001).

An aspect of international mobility which is often overlooked, but is in fact an important learning resource, is what the EU calls "virtual mobility", that is the international nature of class groups for all students and particularly for those who stay at home. The presence of exchange students from many countries in class means that even those students who do not or cannot travel themselves have direct contact with students from a variety of countries and cultures, thus also offering them the opportunity to develop their cultural and intercultural competence. Careful management of this classroom situation by teachers can make it a truly enriching experience for all students involved.

Similarly, virtual student mobility may be achieved by other means, including staff mobility, allowing students to experience teaching and learning activities as they are organized at other institutions, and institutions to incorporate intensive courses in fields in which they do not specialize. As mentioned above, new technologies allow tandem and other forms of cooperative projects to be carried out at a distance, making up at least partially for lack of real physical mobility through contact with students and staff in other institutions and countries.

> To what extent does your institution participate in international mobility programmes? Do all students study for a period abroad? If not, how are programmes organized? How is learning credited? How does this affect your module? For example, are students on exchange programmes expected to take your course at a distance?
>
> How many students from other universities can you expect to have in your classes? From which countries, with which native languages and with what prior knowledge? Will this affect the directionality of your classes? How?
>
> If your module is to be affected by international mobility, write a brief description of how you intend to manage this aspect of teaching and learning. How will you promote the participation of international students? How will you promote home/international student interaction? How will you assess international students? Will they have any special needs you should attend? How will you discover this? (See needs analysis in Chapter 3.)

Work placements

It has become increasingly common in university systems for programmes to credit work experience, including prior work experience for mature students. In some cases, for example on many practice-orientated programmes in France, this work experience is a compulsory element of programmes and institutions offer varying degrees of support to students in the search for a placement, and in follow-up during and after the experience itself. In the field of translation, the incorporation of this kind of experience into training programmes at universities depends to a great extent on the context in which training is taking place, but it probably true to say that almost all programmes offer some form of credit for work experience, whether prior or (much more commonly) acquired during training in some form.

Like mobility programmes, work experience is a rich and complex learning resource which cannot simply be assimilated to traditional classroom learning. As in the case of international exchanges, it is important for placements to take place at an appropriate point in training, normally once students have acquired at least basic translation skills and some knowledge of professional procedures, in particular the basics of computer use applied to translation practice. It is at this fairly advanced stage in training that students have most to gain from engaging in real professional practice. At earlier stages in training, this kind of experience is likely to be excessively complex for students and hence unlikely to produce much meaningful learning.

In work experience, the areas of competence where the student will learn and progress most are the instrumental and professional area (application and appraisal of technology to professional translation; work procedures and flows; professional ethics); the interpersonal area (team work; working relations with other professionals, including revisers); the attitudinal (self-concept as a translator; confidence; taking on responsibility; automatization of professional routines); the strategic area (organization of work flow; problem identification and solving).

In some cases, distinction is made between two different kinds of work placement activity, depending on the stage of learning of the trainee. A first level work placement mostly involves observation, often shadowing a professional tutor, that is accompanying a professional translator permanently and observing what tasks s/he carries out and how they are organized. A second level work placement actually involves the trainee carrying out translation and other tasks, under the direct supervision of a professional tutor, in close collaboration with an academic tutor at the university responsible for the trainee's course. Unfortunately, in most institutions, there are insufficient placements available to ensure that each trainee will have one work experience, let alone two. The two stages can of course, with careful planning, be incorporated into a single work experience, perhaps in two separate periods, the second longer than the first, but with a break to ensure that trainees reflect on what they have observed, prepare questions to eliminate any doubts, plan their participation in the second stage, in order to ensure full benefit will be taken.

If you are working at a university, it is possible that you will be required by your institution to act as a student tutor for work placements in translation companies, translation services in large companies or institutions, whether in the town you work in or further afield. Similarly, if you work at a translation company or service and have responsibility for training, you may be asked to supervise a trainee. In both cases, careful planning of the placement, of coordination between university and company, and of tutorial support for the trainee are all essential elements for the success of this kind of learning activity. Even if you do not have direct responsibility, you may have in your classes students who have undergone this kind of experience and who will have much input to offer the class as a result. You may also have students participating on work placements while they are registered in your module, who require distance tutorial support for the module itself, and who can also offer interesting input to the rest of the class during their work experience.

Does your institution have a work placement programme? Find out how it works and how it may affect or have affected students taking your module. Can you use their experience as input to your module? In what way?

If your institution has no formal system for incorporating work experience to the programme, are there legal constraints preventing it? If not, what can you do to promote this kind of experience for your students? For example, identify and contact local companies and institutions which employ professional translators to discover whether they would be prepared to cooperate with your institution in this way. (Most companies have some form of finance for recruitment, contact with universities and similar activities.)

Even where formal work experience does not exist or is not possible at your institution, there is a wide range of activities which can be carried out to promote student awareness and learning about the profession. The following are only few possibilities, which can also be combined with systematic work placement programmes in training.

- Visits by professional translators to institutions and to individual classes. It is particularly interesting to invite graduates from the programme itself, as this is motivating for students.
- Visits to local translation companies and services, where these exist.
- Analysis of the job market through advertisements published in the specialised professional press or on professional websites such as http://www.proz.com or http://www.aquarius.net.
- Visits by representatives of professional associations.
- Analysis of information available on the websites of professional associations such as ITI (http://www.iti.org.uk), ITIA (http://www.translatorsassociation.ie), BDÜ (http://www.bdue.de), SFT (http://www.sft.fr), ATA (http://www.atanet.org); SATI (http://www.translators.org.za), NZSTI (http://www.nzsti.org), Colegio de Traductores Públicos de la Ciudad de Buenos Aires (http://www.traductores.org.ar), or the Korean Society of Translators (http://www.kstinc.co.kr). The FIT website contains a complete list of member and associate organizations: http://www.fti-ift.org.
- Simulation of professional practice in the classroom: use of translation briefs, use of realistic translation commissions; organization of teams; role play as client, terminologist, translator, researcher, reviser, project manager, layout specialist ...; use of simulated professional workstation,

production of work plans, budgets and invoices, and so on.
- Actual undertaking of professional commission by class groups (with care to pay due respect to local professional norms).

Write a list of local translation companies and services which you could contact as resources for organizing this kind of activity for your module. If there are no or few companies, what other resources can you locate easily for class activities?

Which of the activities listed above are appropriate for your module, given the context and the level at which it is taught? Are there any obstacles preventing you from implementing this kind of activity?

What is/would be the reaction of the local professional community to class groups at your institution taking on real professional commissions? Will this reaction condition your proposing this kind of activity? How?

Identify national translators' associations in your context, and consult their publications and website. Do these constitute useful resources for your module? How can you incorporate them to your teaching?

This chapter has offered a series of ideas relating to resources which may be available to teachers in different institutions. The concept of resources has been interpreted in as broad a sense possible, and more space has been devoted to less obvious resources such as mobility programmes and work experience, precisely because they are valuable resources often under-exploited in translator training. A list of resources and useful websites is given below.

Further reading on resources

Biggs, John (2003) *Teaching for Quality Learning at University. What the Student Does.* Maidenhead: Open University Press [2nd edition: see in particular Chapter 10: "Using Educational Technology: ET not IT"].

Kelly, David (1998) *Effective Speaking.* Huddersfield: Falcon.

Kenny, Dorothy (1999) 'CAT Tools in an Academic Environment: What are They Good For?' *Target,* 11, 1: 65-82.

Kiraly, Donald (2000) *A Socioconstructive Approach to Translator Education.* Manchester: St Jerome. [See in particular Chapter 7 on the computer-based classroom.]

McCarthy, Patsy and Caroline Hatcher (2002) *Presentation Skills. The Essential Guide for Students.* London: Sage.

Pym, Anthony, Carmina Fallada, José Ramón Biau and Jill Orenstein (eds.) (2003) *Innovation and E-Learning in Translator Training.* Tarragona: Universitat Rovira i Virgili. [Part II pp 64-98 is devoted to Translator training and e-learning.]

Teichler, Ulrich and Wolfgang Steube (1991) 'The Logics of Study abroad Programmes and their Impacts'. *Higher Education.* Vol. 21 N°.3. 325-349.

Teichler, Ulrich and Volfer Jahr (2001) 'Mobility during the Course of Study and after Graduation'. *European Journal of Education.* Vol. 36. N° 4. 443-458.

Wisdom, James and Graham Gibbs (1994) *Course Design for Resource Based Learning. Humanities.* Oxford: Oxford Centre for Staff Development.

Interesting websites

On international education and student mobility:

The Academic Cooperation Association http://www.aca-secretariat.be

A bibliography on student mobility will shortly be available at the website of the Temcu Socrates Action 6 Project on training teaching staff for the multicultural classroom arising from mobility programmes: http://www.temcu.com

On work placements:

Support4learning (resources for advisors, students and everyone involved in education, training and communities): http://support4learning.org.uk/careers/work_exp.htm

6. Method: Teaching and Learning Activities

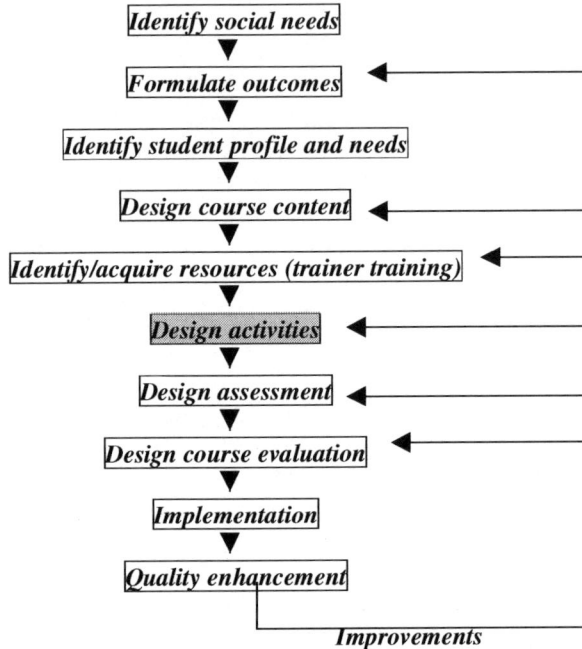

```
              ┌─────────────────────┐
              │ Identify social needs│
              └─────────────────────┘
                        ▼
              ┌─────────────────────┐ ◄───────────────┐
              │ Formulate outcomes  │                 │
              └─────────────────────┘                 │
                        ▼                             │
         ┌──────────────────────────────┐            │
         │ Identify student profile and  │            │
         │          needs                │            │
         └──────────────────────────────┘            │
                        ▼                             │
            ┌─────────────────────┐ ◄─────────────────┤
            │ Design course content│                  │
            └─────────────────────┘                  │
                        ▼                             │
   ┌───────────────────────────────────────┐ ◄───────┤
   │ Identify/acquire resources (trainer    │         │
   │            training)                    │         │
   └───────────────────────────────────────┘         │
                        ▼                             │
            ┌─────────────────────┐ ◄─────────────────┤
            │ Design activities    │                  │
            └─────────────────────┘                  │
                        ▼                             │
            ┌─────────────────────┐ ◄─────────────────┤
            │ Design assessment    │                  │
            └─────────────────────┘                  │
                        ▼                             │
          ┌───────────────────────┐ ◄────────────────┤
          │ Design course evaluation│                 │
          └───────────────────────┘                 │
                        ▼                             │
            ┌─────────────────────┐                   │
            │ Implementation       │                   │
            └─────────────────────┘                   │
                        ▼                             │
          ┌───────────────────────┐                   │
          │ Quality enhancement    │───────────────────┘
          └───────────────────────┘
                        Improvements
```

Summary and aims

This chapter will look at actual **teaching and learning activities**. In particular, the following will be dealt with: types of exercise and activity; **team/group work**; in-class activities vs. activities outside the class; support and **mentoring**. The chapter ends with some examples of contextualized teaching and learning activities for different stages and kinds of training. By the end of this chapter, you should be able to identify different kinds of teaching and learning activity applicable to translator training, and their usefulness at different stages of training; you should be able to establish direct links (alignment) with the learning outcomes you wrote in chapter 2 for your module, bearing in mind the participants (chapter 3) and resources available (chapter 5); you should further be able to design specific teaching and learning activities for the module you are responsible for.

What not to do!

The following is a depressing description of the "traditional" translation class-room, which some students on our local postgraduate programme tell us year after year is still applicable to their own recent undergraduate experience. For-tunately, many others see little or no resemblance between the situation this text describes and their own personal, much richer experience!

> The teacher of the course, a native speaker of the target language, passes out a text (the reason for the selection of this text is usually not explained, because it is often a literary essay that the teacher has just "found" by accident). The text is full of traps, which means that the teachers do not set out to train students in the complex and difficult art of translation, but to ensnare them and lead them into error. The text is then prepared, ei-ther orally or in written form, for the following sessions and then the whole group goes through the text sentence by sentence, with each sen-tence being read by a different student. The instructor asks for alternative translation solutions, corrects the suggested versions and finally presents the sentence in its final, "correct" form... This procedure is naturally very frustrating for the students. (House, 1980: 7-8 cited in Kiraly, 1995: 7)

> Does this quote remind you of your own learning experience as a transla-tor? If so, how did you react as a student to the situation?
>
> Identify aspects of the teaching situation described which you feel are negative. Explain why.
>
> Think of your own teaching: have you designed mechanisms to avoid creating the same sensation of frustration in your students? Which?

Types of teaching and learning activity

In the following section, we will examine some of the most common teaching methods and techniques in higher education, applying them to translator train-ing. The intention is not to opt for any one of them in particular, but rather to comment on their usefulness and potential pitfalls in different contexts and at different levels of training. In general, it is my belief that a well thought-out combination of these techniques, depending on the specific outcomes aimed at and the context, offers the richest learning experience to students and trainees.

Large groups: the lecture or presentation
Large class groups are relatively infrequent in translator training, but this is not

to say that they do not exist or that the **lecture** or large-group presentation does not have a role to play. The lecture has been much criticized as the epitome of teacher-centred approaches, and is thus rejected out of hand by many authors favouring student-centred approaches. This is, I feel, at least partly unfair. There are intended outcomes towards which well organized lectures can contribute. There are also teaching situations in which there is little alternative but to adopt some form of lecturing as a teaching activity. The major problem with lectures is that students can be entirely passive, and that concentration levels drop after some 15 to 20 minutes. It is also the case that a lecture is often understood simply as giving an account of the content which students then automatically acquire. Well-designed lectures which take into account these potential disadvantages by incorporating techniques to make the experience more active and interactive can, however, contribute to student learning.

   Should you decide that you want to give a lecture or presentation to introduce or analyse a particular subject, or should you be teaching in an institutional context which makes lecturing in some form inevitable, here are several points to bear in mind in order to help effective learning actually to take place.

- Where possible, only choose the lecture or presentation when it is the most appropriate activity for the particular outcome sought (essential differences between two legal systems as a basis for the initial stages of legal translation in a group of 100 students, maybe). Remember that you saying something in a lecture does not mean that from that moment on all students will automatically have internalized the point!
- Ensure that the content of the lecture does not correspond simply with reading material easily available to the students. Your role is to select essential points, establish inter-relations, update, and apply content to the learning outcomes, not to transmit content which is readily available in other forms. (Which aspects of legal tradition affect the translator's decision-making process, why and how, not just a comparative history of two legal traditions…). Use practical examples to illustrate abstract theory (actual translation situations in which differences in legal traditions affect translation decisions).
- Link the presentation with prior student reading, but not too much, or too little; make texts for prior reading easily available to students (a brief basic maximum 10-page account of the two legal systems in our example). Make sure that the lecture relates to the reading, but does not simply repeat what students can learn more easily from books or journals. That is, make the reading a pre-requisite for understanding the lecture; that way you doubly ensure learning from reading and application of knowledge acquired from reading to specific outcomes. (Make sure students

are aware of this beforehand, of course; their prior experience of lectures may lead them to believe that it is sufficient to attend and take notes!)

- Use visual support: OHP slides, PowerPoint or similar computer presentations, the blackboard. Prepare handouts which will help students to follow actively (computer presentation software allows you to reproduce slides in the left-hand column of the handout and leave empty space in the right-hand column for student notes, for example). An introduction presenting the overall structure (subheadings), with occasional explicit markers (headings on slides; verbal reminders...) of how far you have advanced, is particularly useful.

- Do not speak for longer than about 15 minutes at a time. Try to ensure some change of activity: a five-minute question time, short small group discussions, answering pre-prepared question sheets, standing up and moving around (if possible!). Some of these activities may be prepared by students before the lecture, based on their reading: ask them to note two or three doubts which arise from the reading which can then be answered in the question session. Research has shown that this brief change of activity allows some recovery of concentration – for a further 15 minutes only, though!

- Remember that most students will be taking notes. Do not speak too fast; make good use of repetition. Occasionally give time for them to note enough detail. This kind of pacing will also help the non-native speakers of the course language amongst them to follow more easily. For the latter, and where possible, avoid also strong accent, regionalisms, culture-bound comment, unless of course dealing with these is one of the intended outcomes...

- Make sure you explicitly relate the content of the lecture to the intended outcomes at the beginning and end of the session. (We are not analysing legal systems in order to be able to practise as lawyers, but to understand the overall context in which legal translation takes place and the implications for text production and translation decisions...) Sum up the main points. Ask students to do the same. This can be done in a variety of ways, the most effective for learning being those which actively involve larger numbers of students. For example, students can be required to write short summaries of content, or reactions to it, in five minutes at the end of the session. Students in pairs or small groups may be asked to summarise or react to lecture content orally to each other. Short questionnaires may be applied. Some of these techniques also allow teachers feedback on how much students have actually learned, and thus allow further action to be taken to ensure sufficient progress towards intended outcomes.

> Identify elements of your module which you believe would best be taught in lecture form. Justify this opinion. Are you sure there are no better alternatives?
>
> If you are sure you need to give lectures for some elements, decide how you could make them more interactive. Choose a topic, and write a short plan for the corresponding lecture session, indicating the steps you will take to ensure quality student learning.

Student presentations

Student presentations are popular on translator training programmes, often as a means of organizing a plenary session in which a particular translation commission and product is analysed from different points of view after individual, pair or small group work. Student presentations have the advantage over lectures that they are more active for the students doing the presentation, but can be just as passive as the traditional lecture for those not presenting (more so, indeed, as students may have less public speaking competence than teachers...). They do have the advantage of allowing acquisition of the valuable generic competence of public speaking, much demanded by employers and little developed on the whole at universities. On courses combining translating and interpreting, presentation skills will of course be doubly important.

The same comments as hold for the traditional lecture above also hold for student presentations, with the difference that teaching and learning activities can be designed specifically to develop the skill. As with other skills, students do not simply learn to make successful presentations by making one, two or three individual or group class presentations a year. These skills are best commented on and performances analysed in small groups, with or without the teacher present.

As with the lecture, student learning from student presentations can be enriched by active involvement on the part of non-presenting students. Apart from the techniques already commented on, an element of peer assessment (see Chapter 8) can be introduced. Written or oral assessment of the content, the translation, activity or reading presented, or the presentation skills demonstrated, can then be made available to the presenting student/s, thus enriching the experience for all.

> On your advanced module, student work groups take turns to present their project work (simulated specialized translation commissions) to the plenary class group. One of the intended outcomes is precisely that of

> improving presentation skills. Think of ways of ensuring this outcome is addressed in the module's teaching and learning activities.
>
> Now think of ways of making listening to peer presentations more active for fellow students on the module.

Small groups

These are probably the most frequent class groups found in translator training, although the exact size will depend on individual institutions and traditions. The reflections which follow are based on situations in which whole groups of anything up to 35-40 students participate. Some texts on small groups would establish a much lower cut-off point (around 20 students), but experience tells us that 35-40 are fairly standard numbers for class groups in translator training, and that the most common techniques used tend to fit into this category. Many of the activities described require further subdivision into **pairs**, or **work-groups** (also known as **syndicates**) of three to five students. This kind of arrangement is also discussed below.

There are a number of standard methods or techniques used with small groups, the following being the most frequent or most useful in translator training.

Brainstorming This consists of spontaneous generation of ideas to foster lateral or creative thinking. It is useful in searching for translation solutions, and in particular to underpin the idea that there is not one "right" answer. It foments creativity in the translation process.

Buzz groups Brief debate on an issue in a group of two or three for subsequent reporting back to the whole class group or plenary. It is very useful in early stages for small specific tasks (aspects of text analysis, identification of problems, identification of possible sources for solutions, comment on proposed solutions...)

Cross-over groups These are groups of three to five students which break up and re-form in a different distribution to ensure transfer of ideas between groups. This may be more useful at later stages of training, when group skills are more highly developed, or for very specific tasks at early stages, such as assessment of how groups function.

Peer-tutoring Students teach and learn from one another. This is an excellent way of taking advantage of different prior knowledge within a class group. International students, for example, or those with other prior studies, may have important input to make to the group as a whole.

Role play Within a small group, roles are assigned to simulate professional situations. One student is the client, another the terminologist, the researcher, the translator, the project manager, the reviser... Care should be taken to ensure that roles are rotated in order to avoid situations in which students who are good at documentary research always end up doing that, and never drafting the translation. They will not improve their drafting skills, nor will the other group members improve their research skills. Notice here also that there is a tendency for the teacher always to take on a role of authority as client, project manager or reviser: this may have its justification in the early stages where it may be difficult for students to do so, but in the later stages there is absolutely no reason why students cannot also play these roles to good effect.

Syndicate *or work group* Normally a group set up to carry out a project (a translation commission) and report back to a plenary class session. This is a frequent technique in translator training, and is compatible with other activities and techniques described above. See also the comment above on student presentations.

> Read back over the different techniques listed above and consider their applicability to your own classroom situation. Using your learning outcomes as a starting point, try to identify which kind/s of activity could be appropriate in working towards each of them in turn for your module or unit.
>
> Which do you think will prove most useful? Most popular? Easiest to put into practice? And which least useful? Least popular? Hardest to put into practice? Why? Note down the problems you see as most likely to crop up on implementing these techniques and think of how you could address each of them.

Reflections on teaching and learning activities

Team/group work

Team work is useful and positive in translator training for several reasons. Firstly, educational research shows that collaborative learning is richer and more effective. Secondly, team work is an important social and personal experience for students. Thirdly, interpersonal skills are not only an important element of professional translator activity, but also an essential generic skill in much demand by employers. Fourthly, small groups prove to be more conducive than large-group activity to the development of high-level cognitive skills such as problem-solving, reasoning or justifying proposals and decisions.

It is, however, essential to remember that interpersonal skills do not simply develop because students are put together in groups! They should be aware of why they are in groups, and what the intended outcomes of their group work are. They should also analyse how their group works, the difficulties arising, and try to find solutions. There are excellent materials available on the market dealing with these issues. See, for example, Gibbs (1995).

In the list of techniques above, different kinds of group and group activity are described briefly. Let us look a little further at some aspects of group formation here.

Pairs or groups? The answer to this will depend on the number of students in the class group, the composition of the class, and the activity planned. In small class groups, pairs may be more appropriate than groups. In class groups with two very marked component subgroups (50% native speakers of the A language and 50% of the B; 50% translators, 50% lawyers on a postgraduate course in legal translation), then again pairs may be particularly appropriate. In pairs, each student has substantial active involvement in tasks set; on the other hand, input is limited in breadth. Brainstorming, for instance, does not work particularly well with only two people for this reason.

How many to a group? Again, class composition may have a considerable influence when determining group size. In a heterogeneous composition (50% home students, native speakers of the A language; 25% international students native speakers of the B language; 25% international students native speakers of neither A nor B, for example), groups of four, where each group is represented more or less proportionally (two-one-one), may be logical, and ensure peer tutoring takes place as different subgroups contribute different prior knowledge. Groups of more than five may get out of hand, particularly when interpersonal and group management skills are not well developed (in the early stages of training). The larger the group, the higher the risk of individual members "hiding" and being able to get away with doing less.

Fixed or variable group composition? Should students form fixed groups or teams at the beginning of a module, or indeed a whole programme, or should they be asked to change group composition during a module or over a programme? On the whole, fixed groups are more suitable in the early stages of training, as they give students time to acquire team skills, analyse how cooperation works, which problems may arise, look for solutions, without the complication of constant changes in personnel. In later stages, variable group composition introduces an element of variety to learning, ensures individual students are exposed to a breadth of situations and approaches, and discourages complacency. For specific activities, cross-over groups are useful. This is particularly the case for the analysis of group working: once a stable work group has analysed its functioning, members re-group with other class members to analyse with greater distance what is going well and what is not, comparing approaches and solutions, which can then be reported back to the original stable work group for action to be taken.

> In your context, which kind of groups do you think are most appropriate for class activity? Think of size, characteristics, and how stable they should be. Will you use different kinds of group for different activities?

Who establishes group composition? All of the above, together with who works with whom, are decisions which may be taken by the teacher, by the students or by teachers and students together. Again, who decides may depend on the stage of training and the intended outcomes, among other circumstances. In particular, deciding who should work with whom in stable groups is a decision best left to the students themselves, with minimum teacher intervention.

> Who will decide on group composition on your module? Why? Identify potential problems.

What do we do when a particular group simply does not work? If, after a trial period and an attempt at analysing and solving internal problems, a work group simply cannot work as a team successfully, there is little point in insisting, and some reshuffling should be allowed. Remember the intended outcome is student learning. If the working environment is such that it prevents students from learning, then a change in that environment is the easiest solution.

> A work group on your module has experienced serious problems with one group member, who attends group meetings only rarely and, when she does, has not prepared the tasks assigned to her and is constantly uncooperative. The other members of the group ask for your help. What do you do?

What about assessment? One of the major reasons for reticence regarding group work in training is its relation with assessment. Teachers are reluctant to use group work as a basis for **summative assessment**, which they believe should be individual. Some, often good students are also reticent, as they feel they miss opportunities for obtaining high grades. These are appropriate criticisms, and the issue of group assessment requires careful consideration and negotiation. It is true that giving the same grade to a whole work group where effort and learning has probably not been shared out equally is problematic. It is similarly problematic, however, to require students to carry out individual assessment tasks if all the course work has been carried out in teams. We deal with this issue in more depth in Chapter 8 on assessment, outlining some of the proposals put forward in the literature, and considering their application to translator training.

> For the moment, note down what you think of using group work as a basis for summative assessment. Have you used it in the past? Has it posed you any problems? Do you think it is fair? If not, in what way is it unfair? We will return to your answers to these points in Chapter 8.

In-class and out-of-class activities

University traditions vary greatly in relation to how much emphasis is placed on what happens inside the classroom during timetabled sessions and what happens elsewhere at other times. At one extreme, formal class contact time is minimal (as little as nine hours a week in some institutions), and students do a great deal of independent study; at the other, students may be in formal classroom situations up to 25 or 30 hours a week, which obviously leaves little time for independent study.

The balance you opt for will obviously take into account your own institutional environment. It is not reasonable to incorporate large amounts of out-of-class activities for students with little free time; you should also remember that you are probably competing with colleagues for that precious time. In this kind of situation, most activity should be programmed for official contact sessions, and other activities carefully coordinated with colleagues to prevent overload. Activity programmed for official contact sessions does not, of course, have to take place in the classroom: the library, the computer room, seminar rooms, the cafeteria, the garden are all possible sites within the institution; which is most appropriate will depend on the activity itself. Similarly, visits (to translation companies for example) and excursions (to attend talks, use resources in other institutions…) are other potential class activities. Nor do all students and the teacher have to be in the same place at the same time: different subgroups may work in different rooms, carrying out different activities, with or without the teacher's presence.

At the opposite extreme, the issues are quite different in nature. Work should be planned to ensure that timetabled sessions can be used for plenary activities, and sufficient contact and support between these sessions should be carefully articulated (email, small group follow-up meetings, individual mentoring…). It may be inappropriate to devote plenary class time to small group work, to visits and excursions.

Where would you situate your institution with regard to class contact time? How many hours a week does a student typically spend in class? What does this imply for your planning? Are there institutional rules which limit the kind of activity you may carry out and where?

If students spend many hours in class, how will you coordinate out-of-class activity with colleagues?

If students have very few contact hours, how will you ensure contact and support between class sessions?

Support and mentoring

Again, on this point, there is a wide range of institutional tradition regarding student support and mentoring outside formal class contact time. Here, we will refer exclusively to academic issues, although the concept of student support is of course much broader, covering personal, social, career, psychological and medical concerns. It is important for you as a teacher to be familiar with the institution's support network in order to point individual students in the right direction should they ask for your help or advice. You cannot be an expert in all kinds of problem and it is much wiser in general to remit the student to those who are. Some institutions will have official protocols for dealing with different kinds of situation which may arise; in other cases, it is a case of individual lecturers deciding. If you give some fore-thought to this, you will avoid improvisation, which is rarely a good counsellor.

Are you aware of your institution's student support network? If not, how can you find out what help is available to students with different kinds of problem?

Does your institution have official guidelines on teaching staff intervention in student problems? Are you familiar with them?

In each of the cases below, decide whether or not you should intervene as a teacher if a student asks for your help. If not, where would you direct the student at your institution?
- ❏ An international student has an urgent dental problem, but is not registered with a dentist in your area.
- ❏ A student in an advanced module confides that a fellow student may have a serious eating disorder, and that she does not know what to do.

> ❑   A final year student requests help in preparing job applications.
> ❑   A recent graduate does not know how much to charge for her first translation commission.
> ❑   A group of first year students are unsure about applying for a scholarship to study abroad during their second year. They ask for your opinion.

With regard to academic support, it is most likely that there will be institutional regulations outlining your obligations in this respect. These may involve "office hours" for all students registered on your module/s, responsibility as a mentor for a small group of students throughout their programme or for a specific period of time, responsibility for a specific area of support on the programme (exchange programmes, work placements, exam organization...), amongst others. Whatever your responsibility, it is essential for students to be aware of how they can contact you, where, and when. It is probably a good idea to make sure that you have some form of individual or at least small group contact with all students as soon as possible on a module. Students will be happier to comment on doubts and ask questions in this setting than in public. Teachers often complain that students do not approach them to discuss doubts. If this is the case, it is extremely simple to organize a round of individual or small-group interviews. It may be that students are not accustomed to speaking personally to teachers, or are reluctant to express doubts openly for fear of appearing not to reach the level expected of them. It is important that they identify you as someone who is there to help them to learn, not as someone who is there constantly to judge and assess their performance. A pleasant atmosphere, ensuring a sufficient degree of privacy and lack of interruption, is essential for this kind of one-to-one or one-to-few attention.

> What do your institution's regulations stipulate about attending individual students outside class? Do you have any specific responsibilities for mentoring at your institution?
>
> How often do individual students come to seek your help or to resolve doubts? If you think they should be seeking help more often, what can you do to encourage them to do so? (Make sure you do not overload your own timetable!)

New technologies, and in particular email, have made asking teachers questions much easier, less time-consuming (for the student) and less threatening. Indeed, so much so that many teachers now find themselves overwhelmed with email messages they simply have not enough time to reply to! In Chapter 5, some suggestions are made as to how to manage this aspect of our teaching activity. Note that, despite its obvious usefulness and efficiency for some communication, email can prove to be distant and impersonal. Care may be needed not to lose sight of the essentially interpersonal nature of teaching as an activity: even when using standard replies, try to personalize them using students' names, for example.

Some examples of teaching and learning activities

To round up this review, let us look at some examples of teaching and learning activities in different training contexts and levels.

Module	Introduction to translation practice
Outcome	Students will be able to identify how cultural differences between source and target text readers may influence translation decisions and propose a range of possible solutions
Activity	Buzz group; mixed nationality groups; strongly culture-bound text; identify implicit information and its importance for the overall communication situation. Reports back to plenary.

Module	Introduction to scientific translation
Outcome	Students will be able to identify and locate suitable documentary resources, and in particular parallel texts and appraise their reliability
Activity	Brainstorming to identify possible resources; plenary reports; each group visits Science Faculty library, uses Internet, visits to experts…. Plenary reports on success. Drawing up of conclusions: protocol for searches, and criteria for reliability.

Module	Advanced level legal translation
Outcome	Students will be able to evaluate their own and peer translations and assess their acceptability as professional products; they will also be able to propose and put in place appropriate measures to ensure quality when working on a free-lance basis.
Activity	Each work group is responsible for assessing at least one other group's translation per session/week/unit. To this end, professional quality report sheets of the kind used by language service providers may used (in adapted form or otherwise). The work is carried out outside the classroom, and then given (anonymously or otherwise) to the group assessed as feedback. This

also involves role-play (one group acts as a team of researchers, terminologists and translators; the other as a team of
revisers).

Situation	End of final year/programme
Overall	Students will be able to carry out specialized translations to
outcome	the standard required of junior translators professionally, in ac-cordance with specific translation briefs and to justify their decisions.
Activity	Individual translation project, independent of specific modules/units. Students choose their own translation commission, write their own (realistic) brief, submit the translation together with an extended commentary on the process (analysis, documen-tary research, terminology, problems encountered, decisions taken, revision…), a full bibliography, and a self-assessment. Staff support (individual or collective supervision) is available throughout. The translation is defended or discussed with a board of at least two members, one of whom may be a fellow student.

Note that the activities described are not intended to ensure, on their own,
full achievement of the outcomes given. They constitute part of an overall module or programme, and as such contribute (in differing degrees) to learning
outcomes.

Now design teaching and learning activities to work towards the following
learning outcomes in the situation given:

Situation	Introduction to professional practice on undergraduate programme
Outcome	Students will be able to discuss and appraise the role of professional translators' associations, particularly those of their immediate local, regional or national context
Activity?	…
Situation	Short professional development course on ethics
Outcome	Participants will be able to analyse situations in which com-plex ethical decisions have to be made, propose potential solutions, and assess those made by colleagues
Activity?	…
Situation	Mid-programme module on audiovisual translation (subtitling)

Outcome	Students will understand the importance of joint visualization of written text and image
Activity?	...
Situation	Beginners' module on translation practice (postgraduate)
Outcome	Students will understand the importance of textual conventions for the translation process, recognize a number of text types and apply knowledge of conventions to specific translation situations
Activity?	...

Using the learning outcomes you wrote for your own module in Chapter 2, design teaching and learning activities for different points in the module (beginning, middle and end).

Try to measure the amount of time students will need (in and out of class) to carry out the activities you have designed. Now ensure that the workload is appropriate for the number of credits/hours you have available for the module.

Finally, think of your own workload. With the activities you are designing, can you cope with the workload you are imposing on yourself (in class time and outside)? Take into account class time, preparation time, time for individual and small-group student support (both in face-to-face meetings and by email and similar), time for assessment activities... It is easy to over-estimate the time we have available, or under-estimate student needs in terms of support.

In this chapter we have commented on different kinds of teaching and learning activity, with emphasis on those appropriate for small groups. Issues relating to team work have been discussed in some detail; less traditional activities outside the classroom have been explicitly included in our repertoire of possible activities; we have stressed the importance of offering individual student support and of encouraging students to make use of support available, while ensuring that teaching staff do not bite off more than they are trained to chew! A similar caveat is made for the design of teaching and learning activities, where it is easy to get carried away and under-estimate the workload we are planning for students and for ourselves! Examples to illustrate teaching and learning activities for different translator training levels and contexts are offered, and readers are encouraged to design their own for their own context. In the next chapter specific issues of sequencing, important in activity design, are dealt with and in Chapter 8 the very important issue of assessment is covered in detail. Returning to our central concept of alignment, both chapters are closely linked to this one, and should be considered together.

Further reading on teaching and learning activities in higher education

Brown, George (1978) *Lecturing and Explaining.* London: Methuen.

Gibbs, Graham (1995) *Learning in Teams. A Tutor Guide.* Oxford: Oxford Centre for Staff Development. [There are also companion publications: *A Student Guide* and *A Student Manual.*]

------, Sue Habeshaw and Trevor Habeshaw (1992) *53 Interesting Things To Do in Your Lectures.* Bristol: Technical and Educational Services.

Habeshaw, Sue, Graham Gibbs and Trevor Habeshaw (1992) *53 Problems With Large Classes.* Bristol: Technical and Educational Services.

Habeshaw, Sue, Trevor Habeshaw and Graham Gibbs (1992) *53 Interesting Things to do in your Seminars and Tutorials.* Bristol: Technical and Educational Services.

Further reading on teaching and learning activities in translator training

The following titles have been selected, from the many available, as they each contain specific proposals for teaching and learning activities. Readers are encouraged also to look at the bibliographical resources listed in Chapter 9, on trainer training, as there is a wealth of material to be found in journals, conference proceedings and other publications.

Colina, Sonia (2003) *Teaching Translation. From Research to the Classroom.* New York, San Francisco: McGraw Hill

Grellet, Françoise. (1991) *Apprendre à traduire. Typologie d'exercices de traduction.* Nancy: Presses Universitaires de Nancy.

González Davies, María (coord.) (2003) *Secuencias. Tareas para el aprendizaje interactivo de la traducción especializada.* Barcelona: Octaedro-EUB

------ (2004) *Multiple Voices in the Translation Classroom.* Amsterdam: John Benjamins.

Hatim, Basil and Jeremy Munday (2004) *Translation. An Advanced Resource Book.* London: Routledge.

Hurtado, Amparo (dir.) (1999) *Enseñar a traducir. Metodología en la formación de traductores e intérpretes.* Madrid: Edelsa.

Kiraly, Don (2000) *A Social Constructivist Approach to Translator Education.*

Empowerment From Theory to Practice. Manchester: St Jerome.

Nord, Christiane. (1991) *Text Analysis in Translation. Theory, Methodology, and Didactic Application of a Model for Translation-Oriented Text Analysis.* Amsterdam: Rodopi. [English translation of Nord, Christiane (1988) *Textanalyse und Übersetzen.* Heidelberg: Groos.]

------ (1996) 'Wer nimmt mal den ersten Satz? Überlegungen zu neuen Arbeitsformen im Überseztungsunterricht'. In Angelika Lauer, Heidrun Gerzymisch-Arbogast, Johann Haller and Erich Steiner (eds.) *Überseztungswissenshaft im Umbruch.* Tübingen: Narr. 313-328. [A detailed critique of the proposals made in this article appears in Kiraly 2000: 54-62. As the critique is in English, it also offers access to the article in English for those who do not read German!]

Robinson, Douglas. (1997) *Becoming a Translator. An accelerated course.* London: Routledge. [2nd edition 2003: *Becoming a Translator. An Introduction to the Theory and Practice of Translation.* See especially the Appendix for Teachers.]

7. Sequencing

```
                    Identify social needs
                            ▼
                    Formulate outcomes  ◄──────────────┐
                            ▼                           │
              Identify student profile and needs        │
                            ▼                           │
               Design course content  ◄────────────────┤
                            ▼                           │
     Identify/acquire resources (trainer training)  ◄───┤
                            ▼                           │
                 Design activities  ◄──────────────────┤
                            ▼                           │
                Design assessment  ◄───────────────────┤
                            ▼                           │
             Design course evaluation  ◄───────────────┘
                            ▼
                   Implementation
                            ▼
                 Quality enhancement
                    └───────────────────────────────────┘
                        Improvements
```

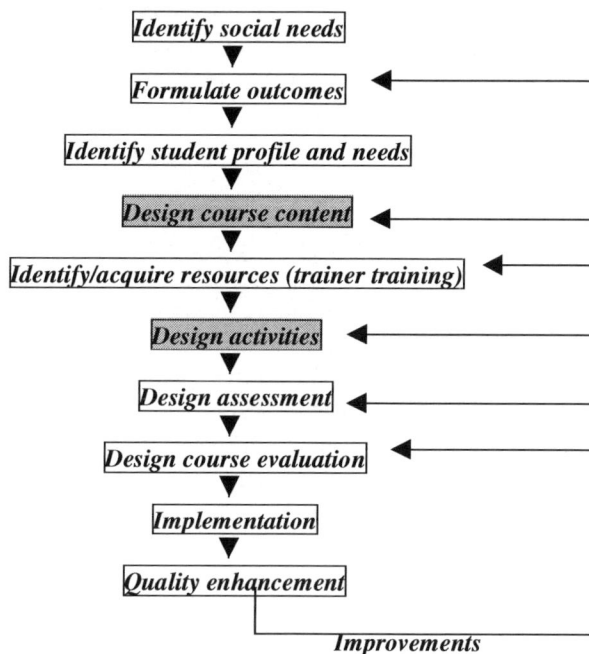

Summary and aims

Now that we have discussed a range of teaching and learning activities for inside and outside the classroom, this chapter will deal with progression. Clearly not all activities are suitable for all levels of learning, and it is in general up to the teacher to decide which are most appropriate for each stage. We will start the chapter with some brief general considerations on long-standing issues relating to **sequencing** such as whether theory or practice should come first, or language skills and their acquisition prior to translator training or simultaneous with it; we will then move on to discuss the sequencing of types of activity or exercises. Finally the question of selecting texts for translation practice is addressed, and a series of possible criteria for selection is suggested. Last but not least, we will discuss how to involve trainees in the selection of materials. By the end of the chapter, readers should be able to identify criteria appropriate to their own context for the selection of activities and texts for class use.

Before going into any detail on the different points to be covered in this chapter, it is perhaps appropriate to return to our systematic curricular design strategy, and to remember that whatever we do in the classroom or in the teaching and learning process in general will depend on our aims, the intended learning outcomes of the particular stage of the training process, and the context in which we are working (with which students, in which social, economic, institutional context, with which resources at our disposal…). Any doubts over the priority of one criterion for sequencing over another can usually be resolved by returning to this very basic premise.

Theory/practice

There has been longstanding debate over which should come first: theory or practice. This is, of course, closely linked to the teaching and learning styles discussed in chapter 3. Some learners will prefer deductive approaches, using theory to solve practical problems. Others will prefer to proceed inductively, reaching conclusions regarding general principles for solving problems from actual problem-solving. There seems to be fairly extensive consensus today that inductive approaches encourage deeper learning. The teacher cannot forget, however, that there will be differences in individual approaches to learning within any group of students, and that, if we take the Kolb learning cycle (see figure 6) as a model, all learners must go through all stages in order for real significant learning to take place. The difference is to be found in the starting point on the cycle. In fairness to the range of students and their learning styles, it is probably advisable not to adopt one single strategy for all activities, and to adopt a flexible approach allowing different learners to apply their own personal styles.

> How would you define your own learning style? Which do you consider to be the dominant learning style in your social and institutional context?
>
> For the particular module or course you are going to teach, have the students received any prior theoretical background? How and in which context (another module, content on a previous practical module, readings…)? In what way will this affect the activities you undertake in your module?

In translation, there is also longstanding debate between academia and the profession with regard to the usefulness of theory for translation practice. Much of this debate arises because of the profusion of theoretical work on literary translation, which now represents a very small percentage of professional translations, and is perceived to involve problems quite different in nature to those faced by technical or legal translators, localizers, and so on. This perception may or may not be "true", but is in any case unhelpful. There has been much research into translation in the past fifty years which is of use to the practitioner, but is possibly couched in inaccessible form, or distributed in restricted circles. There is also a clear need for more research to be carried out in areas which can actually facilitate the practitioner's task. For a very interesting representation of this debate, Chesterman and Wagner (2002) makes good reading, whichever "side" of this divide you approach the issue from.

> What is your own opinion of the role of translation theory in translator training? And of its usefulness for the profession? Will these opinions influence the design of your course/module? In what way?

Language learning/translation

Much translator training, particularly at undergraduate level, is based on the myth that learners already master their "working languages". I use the term myth because the vast majority of translator trainers are aware that the future translators they are working with simply do not have the language competence necessary to undertake many translation tasks, particularly at the beginning of their training. Although there are differences from one context to another, there does seem to be a common denominator in this respect in much undergraduate translator training. It is much less so, for obvious reasons, in postgraduate courses. As individual trainers, there is normally little we can do to remedy the overall situation, at least in the short term. What we can do is to make sure that the activities we design, and the order in which we put them into practice, are in consonance with a realistic appraisal of the language level of our students. It is particularly unhelpful for all involved, in my opinion, to perpetuate the pretence that things are as they should ideally be, when they manifestly are not.

> How would you describe the language level of the students entering your module/course (both working languages involved in the learning process)? Does it correspond to the level expected of them? How will this situation affect the design and sequencing of activities on the module/course in your case?

Sequencing of activities: tasks and projects

Linked to the issue of language competence, although wider in scope, is the tendency for translator training proposals regarding types of teaching and learning activities to be rather monolithic; that is, little attention seems to be paid to the level at which learning is taking place. As we have seen, in order for a translation programme to be fully aligned, teaching and learning activities should fit in, not only with intended outcomes, but also with student profiles, which naturally vary from level to level. Thus, an appropriate approach to the advanced level of training, for example, may be that advocated by Vienne (1994), Gouadec (2000), or Kiraly (2000): the so-called "situational" or project-based approach, where an entire student group assumes responsibility for an authentic or realistically simulated large-scale translation commission, thus coming across real translation problems in a real or realistic context, in all its multi-facetted complexity. But large-group project work of this kind is not, in all probability, the best way to go about the early acquisition of many of the non- specifically translational competences which are prerequisites for the translational. Spanish educationalist Gros Salvat (1995: 187) reminds us that acquiring expertise is not just a matter of reproducing what experts do and know in the classroom. Interesting recent and reflective approaches for this earlier stage of learning are, for example, task-based proposals, taking as the starting point for each activity very detailed intended learning outcomes. Hurtado (1999) and González Davies (2003 and 2004) give detailed descriptions of this approach to translator training (although they themselves do not limit its scope to the early stages of training). This kind of approach allows for careful monitoring of student learning in small gradual steps, ensuring that all steps are covered, and allowing detailed feedback on progress. Detailed planning and close coordination of these early stages in each of the areas of competence mentioned in chapter 2 lay a strong foundation for the student autonomy required for the complexity of advanced large-scale collaborative project work. Clearly, it is much more effective for this coordination to take place at institutional level, as isolated attempts at innovation on individual modules, although useful and praiseworthy, cannot offer a guarantee of overall coherence in training.

These two major approaches (projects versus tasks) are sometimes seen as antagonistic. It is my belief that they are, rather, complementary, and that the difference between them is simply a question of level/stage of training, that is of sequencing. In this respect, rather than two opposing paradigms, they are perhaps better understood as the two extremes of a cline related to student autonomy, thus:

Task-based approaches   **Project-based approaches**

──────────────────────────────────▶

Increasing student autonomy

Figure 12. Student autonomy and appropriate teaching approaches

An important and often neglected point here, then, is that sequencing does not only affect content (what we do/learn/translate), but also and perhaps more essentially, method (how we do/learn/translate).

> Where would you situate the students/trainees you will be working with on this cline of student autonomy? Which kind of approach do you believe is more appropriate for the particular stage you are dealing with. Why?

Criteria for text selection

Let us hope that the rather frustrating situation described by House and which we reproduce at the beginning of Chapter 6 is no longer applicable to how texts are selected in translator training today. It may, however, still be true that criteria are sometimes not explicit or entirely appropriate. It is also probably true that we have all as trainers had the experience of selecting texts which then do not "work" well with learners.

> Can you remember an occasion when a text you selected for class did not work well? Can you identify the reasons for that?

As we have seen so far in this chapter, sequencing and hence selection of materials and texts are complex issues dependent on a variety of factors. Crucial are the characteristics of the students or trainees themselves, and the intended learning outcomes. Moving on from there, this main section of the chapter will begin with a very brief selective review of what some TS authors have written about text selection, and then propose a series of general criteria which may be applied.

Hurtado (1995:60) offers four basic criteria (types of interest) on which to base the selection of texts, which she links to the objectives she proposes for the initial level of training (summarized here using her terminology):

- Linguistic interest (she associates this criterion with what she calls contrastive objectives)
- Extra-linguistic interest (associated with complementary cognitive objectives, tools and thematic fields)
- Text typological interest (objectives linked with text typology, which she situates at the end of the initial stage of training)

• Interest from the point of view of understanding the mechanisms of the
translation process (related to methodological objectives, essentially at
the earliest stage of training).

Nord (1991: 147) reminds us that:

> [s]electing texts for translation classes is not a matter of adhering to rigid
> principles – particularly if one is looking for authentic material, which
> has not been produced for didactic purposes and which therefore often
> resists schematization. Nor is it a matter of mere intuition.

She then proceeds to establish a classification of types of difficulty encountered
in translating:

• Text-specific difficulties (degree of "comprehensibility" of the source
text, related to the intra-textual factors of text analysis)
• Translator-dependent difficulties (related to the level of the learner's
knowledge and competence)
• Pragmatic difficulties (related to the nature of the translation task)
• Technical difficulties (related to research and documentation) (*ibid.*: 152-5)

This classification of difficulties leads her to the following considerations on
the type of texts which should be used at the early stage of training:

> At the basic level, we start working with highly conventionalized,
> transcultural or universal text types, whose constellation of factors al-
> lows little variation, and whose intratextual features are conventional
> (text-specific difficulties). These texts should deal with subject matters
> belonging to the students' sphere of personal experience, and the ST text-
> type conventions should be familiar to the students. The TC conventions
> of the target culture should be rather rigid and known to the translators
> (translator-dependent difficulties). The translation skopos should be de-
> fined in detail by unambiguous translating instructions, and require the
> preservation of situational factors (pragmatic difficulties). The source-
> text should be free of faults and presented in its original form, and the
> teacher should provide sufficient TL auxiliary material (parallel and model
> texts) (= technical difficulties). (*ibid*: 156)

Finally in this brief review, Kussmaul (1995: 51) adds a motivational factor
to the previous considerations:

> ...then students should be able to take a positive attitude toward their
> task. They should like their text (and maybe their teacher) or at least
> should like translating it. The problem must not appear too big for them,

nor too simple either. As teachers, we should take care to select texts with an appropriate degree of difficulty for the specific stage of translator training.

> These considerations from leading authors on translator training offer some basic criteria to be taken into account when selecting texts (and activities in the case of Nord). Write a list of criteria you believe to be appropriate for the level and kind of module you are working with. You will then be able to compare it with the suggestions made below and design a set of criteria appropriate to your own context.

As we have seen, many authors insist on professional realism as an essential pillar for translator training. We mention above the situational approach, for example. In my opinion, professional realism is a key element which, however, should be carefully combined with progression in the learning process. From this point of view, the selection of texts and activities will be based on a careful combination of different criteria, always depending on the particular stage of training. In general, criteria relating to professional realism take on greater importance in later stages of training, whereas others linked to pedagogical progression will prevail in the early stages. The following is a list of criteria based partially on the literature and partially on my own classroom experience. It is offered as a starting point for reflection, not a one-size-fits-all model; you will no doubt need to adapt it to your own context.

a. Professional realism

i. Authenticity of texts and other material
Consensus in the field is that texts should, as far as possible, be authentic, un-manipulated and presented in their original form. The latter in particular allows aspects such as the inter-relation of verbal and non-verbal elements, or formal issues such as how to reproduce figures and tables to be dealt with. In this same vein, texts should be complete. As it is almost inevitable to translate only excerpts, given the time available and the difficulty involved in finding short texts which fulfil the remaining criteria, whenever possible the whole text from which the excerpts are taken should be made available, in order to ensure that textual features are fully taken into account.

A point worth remembering here is that these suggestions for criteria are intended to be flexible, and in particular to work in combination with each other and with the overriding criterion of intended learning outcomes. On occasion, for example, the omission of a particularly complicated fragment of text is perfectly justifiable at an early stage of training, as is minor manipulation of texts for specific (often pre-translation) activities. It is still nonetheless the case that real texts are the most appropriate material for class activities. Fortunately, new technologies have made finding real texts appropriate for specific outcomes much easier than it was only ten years ago.

> Do you share this very generally mooted, but perhaps less commonly practised, criterion? Why (not)?
>
> Have you ever felt the need to manipulate an authentic text for use in class? For what reason? What kind of manipulation? Was this the only solution, or could the text have been replaced by a similar one? Could the activity have been adapted (instead of the text) to allow the use of the original authentic and un-manipulated text?

ii. Realism of the translation situation

The texts selected should respond to characteristics which give rise to at least one realistic translation situation. Thus, translating what's on at the local cinema or very local news is unlikely to be realistic in most contexts, especially in essentially monolingual social environments. This criterion also implies realism in relation to the language combination, and the frequency of text types translated in different directions. Source texts which are themselves translations, for example, are only appropriate when there is a likelihood that they would be used as sources for relay translation professionally (often the case of English, for example; see Dollerup 1997), or where the intended outcome of the exercise is related to back-translation as a translational practice (in very few real situations!).

This second criterion works very much in favour of texts which offer more than one possible translation situation. These allow a variety of activities where students are required to work with different translations of the same source text in different situations, thus helping to consolidate the premise that there is not only one correct translation for each source text. One example might be the translation of a scientific paper for publication in a journal, and translating the same paper to help a scientist to understand the content which may be applicable to her own research work.

> Think of examples of texts which do not meet the criterion of realistic translation situation for your language combination. Do you agree that they are not appropriate for class use? If not, think of situations when

> you might use them, and justify your opinion.
>
> Think of an example of a source text for which there are at least two possible realistic translation situations.

iii. Professional ethics

The issue of ethics is often entirely absent from training programmes. Where it is included, it is often in the form of an isolated seminar, and prominence is given to protecting the profession and/or the market (dealing with issues such as rates, undercutting, and so on). In my opinion, ethical questions should be present throughout training, both explicitly and implicitly, and understood in the broadest possible sense (the translator's social responsibility, ideological manipulation of text and so on). One way of ensuring their presence is through (explicit) text selection criteria. If a particular activity is not considered ethical in the professional context for which we are training, our criterion might be, for example, to exclude it from training; another might be to include it in order to analyse or question standard practice.

> One particular issue where professional codes of conduct are often at odds with practice is that of directionality. Training programmes usually include translating in both directions (into and out of native language): what implications does this have?
>
> Can you think of examples of texts or activities which should be excluded from training programmes in your context in accordance with a criterion of professional ethics?

iv. Professional market

Texts and activities chosen should reflect in general the real professional market trainees are heading for, whether it be local, regional, national or global. This implies knowledge of that market and major trends existing (see chapters 2 and 5) on the part of trainers. In my own institution, for example, some weight is given to texts produced and translated in the tourist sector, of major importance for the local, regional and national economy. By the same token, localization is a major element for students working out of English, but is not covered into English, nor does it receive the same attention for language combinations in which English is neither source nor target language.

> To what extent should the professional market determine the selection of texts for training?

> Is it still feasible to speak of a local market in today's globalized world? If you think the concept is still applicable, which texts are most translated locally in your context? Should they be incorporated into your training programme? At what stage?

These four criteria relating to professional realism allow students to associate what they do during training with real professional activity, thus contributing to the development of what Kiraly (1995, 2000) calls their "self-concept" as translators. Clearly, when applied to text selection, the criteria also help ensure that trainees find the transition to the world of work easier, as the activities are similar and hence familiar, at least to some degree. They are, however, in my view, insufficient as a guide to text selection for the learning process, in that there is no concept of progression, and little attention is paid to the learners' prior experience and knowledge. The second set of criteria (which I have brought together under the heading pedagogical progression) is designed precisely to take these elements into account.

b. Pedagogical progression

i. Text types
Texts selected should be representative of the main genres and sub-genres present on the professional market, and organized from the most highly conventionalized to the least, from the most formulaic to the least. In this vein, Hatim and Mason (1997) propose a double scale of evaluativeness and markedness. Thus, texts with very obvious features and conventions, such as recipes, letters, or weather reports are the most appropriate for the early stages of training, moving on to less static and increasingly dynamic texts; creative texts such as literary texts of all kinds or certain forms of advertising, are situated at the other end of the scale.

The same authors propose establishing the order of text types according to their rhetorical purpose, beginning with instructive texts, moving on to expositive and finally ending with argumentative texts. Other authors (Reiss 1976, Newmark, 1988, Reiss, Nord 1988/1991) use Buhler's classification of expressive, informative and vocative functions (they use different terminologies, but with no difference in meaning), the most appropriate for the early stages being informative, followed by vocative, moving on finally to the expressive.

> This criterion seems to enter into conflict with the received knowledge that "general" translation should precede "specialized" translation on

December 19
E exilada.

> ng programmes, in that texts known as general are often highly dy-
> in nature. What is your opinion? What does "general" translation
> Is it a useful category for training?
>
> of some more specific examples of texts which are suitable for
> early stages of training, in accordance with this criterion. And for an
> intermediate stage?

ii. Prototypical discourses

Alongside text types as such, it is important in my view to try to include texts in which the macrodiscourses of the trainees' different working cultures can be identified and analysed from the point of view of intercultural communication. As we mentioned in our discussion of translator competence in Chapter 2, future translators need to be aware of the macrodiscourses arising from values and myths which underlie and inform a culture's texts. Knowledge of and strategies for dealing with cultural differences in macrodiscourses of questions such as privacy, or different taboos, constitute key elements in the translator's cultural and intercultural competence, and must appear in training. Similarly, the macrodiscourses of sexism, racism, social exclusion allow analysis of issues relating to the translator's ethical position and social role. It is all too easy to reproduce only majority discourse on these questions in training (perhaps even more so in interpreting than in translating), avoiding critical analysis.

> For your particular language combination, which cultural macrodiscourses do you consider should be covered by selected texts? What kind(s) of text are most appropriate for illustrating these macrodiscourses? Do they also fulfil other criteria mentioned?

iii. Content accessibility

Class material in general should reflect progression in content, starting with content related to learners' previous experience both in general and in text use, and moving on towards content with which they have had no life or text experience. This is probably what many trainers and writers mean when they speak of the evolution from "general" to specialized translation. As I have mentioned above, the concept of "general" translation is particularly unhelpful, as it is essentially a non-category. It is much more useful to conceive of texts as fitting into levels of specialization in communication. Arntz (1988) speaks of three basic levels: non-specialist (sender) to non-specialist (receiver); specialist (sender) to non-specialist (receiver); specialist (sender) to specialist (receiver).

It is also conceivable to add the category of non-specialist (sender) to specialist (receiver) (an eyewitness addressing a lawyer or a judge). In fact, in general it is probably more appropriate to conceive of degrees of specialization in communication on a double sliding scale, where the horizontal scale represents degree of specialization, and the arrows on the vertical axis represent actual texts, thus:

Sender

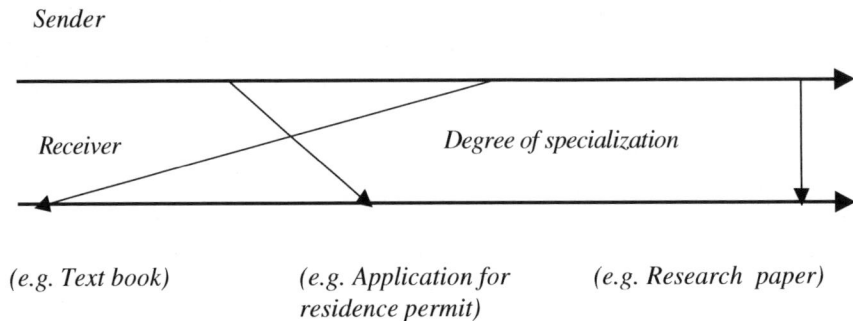

(e.g. Text book)   *(e.g. Application for*   *(e.g. Research paper)*
                                residence permit)

Figure 13. Degrees of specialization

Normally, trainees' text experience is limited to the lower levels of specialization, the left hand side of the scale, both as receivers and even more so as senders. It seems to make sense to take this into account when selecting texts, as in this way there is less risk of more complex levels of content interfering with the already complex operation of translating. To commence translation activities for 19-year-old undergraduates with contracts or similarly complex documents of which they have little or no personal experience is to bring unnecessary obstacles into play. Most trainees will be familiar with recipes, letters, student information leaflets, tourist information, press articles, all of which fulfil other criteria for text selection and are useful at the early stage.

Progression in relation to accessibility should take into account that the older students become, the wider their life experience in general; similarly, academic activities such as exchange programmes widen their field of experience; other course modules taken will widen their knowledge in broad thematic areas (e.g. options in Economics, Law, Science or Technology); finally, as they progress on their course, they will acquire increasing capacity for documentary research (see iv. Below).

Accessibility of content is an interesting issue at later stages of training, where there has been considerable debate as to whether, for example, Scientific Translation courses should attempt to cover many different disciplines, or rather concentrate on one field (say Physiology) and deal with it in depth by working with many different text types within the same subject area. The criterion of accessibility would tend to favour the second option, as continuity in content allows trainees to deal with different translation problems in depth without having to devote much time to repeating basic documentary research and comprehending essential concepts, as would be the case if in week 1 they had to deal with Physiology, in week 2 with Histology, in week 3 with Palaeontology and so on. After all, it is impossible on any training programme to cover all the possible thematic fields in which translation takes place professionally. Our training courses are intended to help students acquire skills which may then be generalized and extrapolated to the many different professional situations they may find themselves in.

Based on their double scale of markedness and evaluativeness, Hatim and Mason (1997: 188 ss) suggest that an international treaty is a suitable text type for the initial stages of training. Evaluate this proposal in the light of this criterion of accessibility of content.

With regard to later stages in training, does your institution have a policy regarding which fields should be covered in specialised translation? If so, what is the basis of that policy? How does the criterion of accessibility of content relate to it?
If not, which of the two approaches mentioned do you favour? Why?

---

iv. Accessibility of reliable documentation
This point is closely linked to iii. above and to vi. below. Documentary research skills are essential for professional translators, but trainees do not usually have them in the early stages of training. It is important, for that reason, for initial texts to require little research, or for the research required to be relatively simple. Trainers can, initially, provide support in different forms: material on paper; information sessions with experts; sessions in the computer room with guided searches to ensure reliable sources are identified, for example. This helps students to identify quality sources, and to establish ways of measuring reliability. It is, however, important for trainers to withdraw this support gradually, in order to guarantee that trainees will be able to work with increasing autonomy. It is interesting to note that in this aspect of professional activity, access to the Internet has brought about a radical change for translators. The change is not, unfortunately, problem-free: translators and trainees now have an overwhelming amount of information at their disposal, and need sound criteria to determine the reliability of the different sources. Trainers' efforts must, therefore, aim at developing discernment.

Think of, or find, an example of a text (type) where little or no documentary research is required.

> Now think of, or find, a text (translation commission) for which some
> rudimentary research skills are required. Design class activity with this
> text for an early stage of training, deciding which documentation you
> will provide the students, and in which form. What kind of activity can
> students carry out in order not only to produce a translation of the text,
> but also to improve their incipient research skills, in particular in relation
> to identifying reliable sources?

v. Student interest and motivation.

In Chapter 3, the issue of motivation is discussed at some length. Kussmaul
reminds us in the quote above of its importance in text selection, as does Nord
(1991:157). This criterion is related to iii., accessibility of content, but is not
identical. Accessibility of content refers to students' prior experience and knowledge; their interest or liking for the texts they work with is more subjective, and
probably much more varied. It is, in any case, predictable that certain subjects
are of more interest to the majority of students than others. Music, cinema, sport,
local places of interest or events, social service or non-profit making organizations may be some examples. It is not my suggestion that an entire beginners'
module be based on texts from these fields or on these subjects, as this would
enter into direct contradiction with several other criteria given here, particularly
with regard to professional realism, but rather that a few texts on each be taken
as the basis for different activities and exercises as an incentive to promote
more active learner participation. Even within these areas, it is important to
ensure variety, in an attempt to respond to the interests of as many individual
students as possible, and to avoid boredom from repetition.

At later stages in training, professional realism itself becomes a motivating
element, as learners see their transition to the world of work closer, but in the
early or even intermediate stages (depending on the length of the course), the
profession seems too far away to most learners for it to constitute immediate
motivation.

> Identify two or three fields of interest to your students, and then related
> text types. Are they suitable for initial translation activities? Do they ful-
> fil other criteria, in particular those relating to professional realism? If
> not, would their use still be justified in your opinion?

vi. Feasibility

Closely related to the previous criterion of motivation is that of feasibility. Texts
and particularly activities selected must be feasible for students. As Kussmaul

comments in the quote above, they should be neither too difficult nor too easy. Over-difficult texts and activities can only discourage learners; over-simple activities are de-motivating as no challenge is involved and nothing new is learnt. Feasibility is not only a question of the difficulty "inherent" to the task at a particular stage of training, but also of the conditions in which the task is to be carried out: deadlines, technical questions such as different electronic formats for submission, and so on. Trainers can make an otherwise simple task much more demanding (and hence motivating) by requiring it to be carried out in a very short period of time (with the aim of encouraging advanced students to learn to work at speed, as required professionally) or in a previously unknown format. Similarly, an initially complex task may be simplified and made feasible by adapting quality requirements (draft translation for revision, instead of final publishable version; working document for internal use only; a summary or an on-sight oral translation for information only), or working conditions (group work or pair work instead of individual preparation).

Can you think of other ways of increasing or decreasing the difficulty of translation tasks in order to ensure an appropriate level of task feasibility?

One of my colleagues suggests that the occasional use of unfeasible translation commissions in class helps students acquire awareness of their limitations, and thus very necessary caution for their future professional practice. Appraise this proposal.

Trainee involvement

These criteria, which are intended essentially and initially to be useful to trainers, may be put to other uses. If made transparent and explicit to trainees, they encourage trainee understanding and hence more active involvement.

A final word on who should be responsible for text and activity selection. In traditional teacher-centred environments, there is no doubt as to the answer to that question: the teacher or trainer. In some environments, decisions may even be taken at a higher institutional level (department, school...). But within a more student-centred paradigm, there is no reason (indeed quite the opposite) why students should not choose at least some, if not all of the texts they are to translate. This may be done in a variety of ways, again depending on the stage of training.

It is particularly difficult for beginners to choose their own material as they are unaware of the problems involved. But that does not mean they should be excluded from all decisions on class activity. At this stage, trainee involvement

may be achieved by the trainer offering a range of carefully selected texts and
activities from which students may choose, within certain limits (one each from
a series of categories, for example), either collectively or individually. In this
way, students identify more with activities, feel more in control of their own
learning, and are more motivated. At later stages in training, it is conceivable
for students to choose up to 100% of the texts and activities to be worked with
in class, usually within parameters established by the trainer or the class collectively as to text type, length, subject matter, kind of activity and so on. The
activity of text selection is a rich learning experience which encourages students to acquire greater awareness of translation problems, and to reflect on
different professional activities, with their relative difficulty. It also encourages
learner autonomy and the taking on of responsibility, especially when the task
in question is to be carried out by the whole class group, not just the individual
student. In successive years in their end-of-module assessments, students on a
final year module at my institution choosing their own texts and writing their
own translation commissions, have identified this aspect as one of the most
enjoyable and motivating of the module. I can also confirm that they have selected a range of demanding and interesting texts, and designed very realistic
and feasible translation commissions. The fear many trainers have that trainees
will simply look for "easy" texts to ensure good marks, or that trainees have
insufficient criteria on which to base their selection has certainly not been con-
firmed by this experience.

> What is your opinion of students selecting their own translation commis-
> sions, or other learning activities?
>
> Can you think of ways in which students on your module could partici-
> pate in the selection of their own activities and/or material? Comment on
> how their level of training and prior knowledge/experience affects this
> involvement.

This chapter has discussed sequencing from different points of view. In particular, the point has been made that sequencing affects not only content or texts for
translation, but also activities to be carried out. A set of criteria for text selection has been put forward, with the caveat that context, intended outcomes and
student profiles constitute overriding criteria for all aspects of course design.
Finally, readers are encouraged to consider the possibility of students assuming
different degrees of responsibility for the selection of texts and class activities.

Further reading

Chesterman, Andrew and Emma Wagner (2002) *Can Theory Help Translators? A Dialogue Between the Ivory Tower and the Wordface.* Manchester: St Jerome.

Hatim, Basil and Ian Mason (1997) *The Translator as Communicator.* London: Routledge.

Hurtado Albir, Amparo (1995) 'La didáctica de la traducción. Evolución y estado actual'. In José María Bravo Gozalo and Purifiación Fernández Nistal (coords.) *Perspectivas de la traducción inglés/español.* Valladolid: ICE, Universidad de Valladolid. 49-74 [especially pages 59-62]

Nord, Christiane (1991) *Text Analysis in Translation. Theory, Methodology, and Didactic Application of a Model for Translation-Oriented Text Analysis.* Amsterdam: Rodopi. [English translation of Nord, Christiane (1988) *Textanalyse und Übersetzen.* Heidelberg: Groos: see particularly pp 147-160.]

8. Assessment

```
                    ┌─────────────────────┐
                    │ Identify social needs│
                    └─────────────────────┘
                              ▼
                    ┌─────────────────────┐
                    │ Formulate outcomes  │ ◄──────────────┐
                    └─────────────────────┘                │
                              ▼                             │
              ┌───────────────────────────────┐            │
              │ Identify student profile and needs│        │
              └───────────────────────────────┘            │
                              ▼                             │
                    ┌─────────────────────┐                │
                    │ Design course content│ ◄─────────┐   │
                    └─────────────────────┘            │   │
                              ▼                         │   │
          ┌─────────────────────────────────────┐      │   │
          │ Identify/acquire resources (trainer training)│ ◄──┤
          └─────────────────────────────────────┘          │
                              ▼                             │
                    ┌─────────────────────┐                │
                    │ Design activities   │ ◄─────────┐    │
                    └─────────────────────┘           │    │
                              ▼                        │    │
                    ┌─────────────────────┐            │    │
                    │ Design assessment   │ ◄──────────┤    │
                    └─────────────────────┘            │    │
                              ▼                        │    │
                  ┌───────────────────────┐            │    │
                  │ Design course evaluation│ ◄────────┘    │
                  └───────────────────────┘                 │
                              ▼                              │
                    ┌─────────────────────┐                 │
                    │ Implementation      │                 │
                    └─────────────────────┘                 │
                              ▼                              │
                  ┌───────────────────────┐                 │
                  │ Quality enhancement   │─────────────────┘
                  └───────────────────────┘
```

Improvements

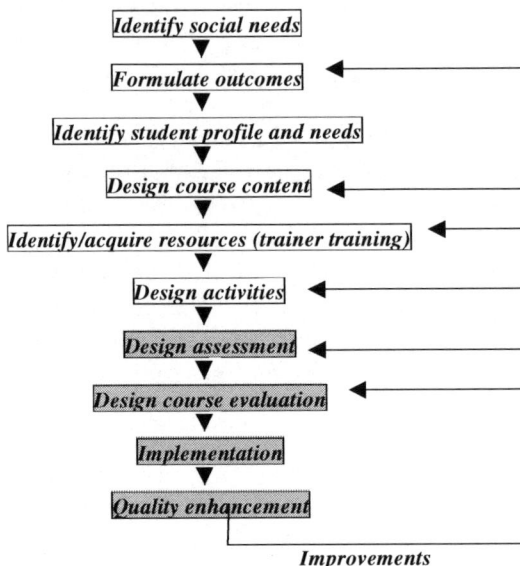

Summary and aims

This chapter will close our systematic approach to curricular and syllabus planning and design. Assessment, in its many forms and with its different functions, is an essential part of any teaching and learning process. Most emphasis has been put traditionally on its **summative** function, but we will stress here the **formative** function. The chapter begins with a critique of traditional assessment methods in translator training, and moves on to discuss principles of student-centred assessment, and a variety of innovative methods, including **peer** and **self assessment** or **learning portfolios**, which may be used alone or in combination with each other to improve assessment practice. **Norm and criterion-referenced grading** practices are then compared, and some suggestions are given as to how to formulate **assessment criteria**. Finally the chapter closes with issues relating to assessment of trainer performance and **programme evaluation**. This really does bring us full circle: feedback from these last provides input for course improvement and **quality enhancement**. By the end of the chapter, readers will have received a broad overview of the concepts of assessment, well beyond standard end-of-semester grading, and should be able to propose and adopt appropriate assessment mechanisms for their own modules in their own contexts.

The evaluation of translations and the concept of error

> Define a good translation. Now, define translation error.
>
> As you will realize in writing these definitions, these are difficult concepts to define and concepts on which there is not overall consensus in TS. But, in what way are these definitions useful for your teaching? And for assessment of student learning?

"The assessment of translator performance is an activity which, despite being widespread, is under-researched and under-discussed" (Hatim and Mason, 1997: 197). Indeed, the question of translation quality and assessment is unanimously recognized as being of great importance, both in the profession and in training. Within the profession different classifications and scales for the evaluation of translations as products have been drawn up and are used on a daily basis; reference is made to these in the further reading section. For the purposes of this chapter, let us underline two of their essential features: on the one hand, they tend to centre on the concept of translation error; on the other, there is no real overall consensus on what constitutes an acceptable translation. In training, assessment is an activity which we as teachers carry out regularly, and for which we often turn to professional practice for guidance. In the discussion which follows, we will examine and question some general trends in assessment in training contexts, and attempt to lay some foundations for sounder practice.

Traditional assessment on translator training programmes

> How are translation modules usually assessed in your institution? Are there agreed criteria for grading? Who is responsible for the setting of criteria and for the actual assessment of individual modules: the teacher, a team of teachers, external examiners, others?
>
> Is this system the most appropriate, in your opinion? Note down elements of the system you are unhappy with, and give reasons.

Traditional assessment on translator training programmes, and indeed for recruiting professionals at international organizations or for membership of some professional associations, takes the form of a translation examination paper, consisting of writing a translation of an unknown text, with or without dictionary/ies, in a limited period of time in a typical examination environment. Correction is based on counting up the errors, often subtracting points for each of them from a notional "perfect" version worth 10/10, 20/20, 100% depending on the national tradition of marking scales. This kind of tests may be criticized from a variety of perspectives, which we sum up here.

- They are unrealistic, that is they have little or nothing to do with real professional translation situations (prior knowledge of type of text, subject area, possibility for documentary research of all kinds, kind of time pressure, physical environment...).
- They attempt to measure all the skills making up the translator's overall competence at once; they further assume that the product is a fair indication of each of these skills, many of which are process, not product related (Hatim and Mason 1997: 198).
- Criteria for examination text selection are often obscure, unclear, or in the worst cases, practically non-existent.
- They show intrinsic lack of faith in students' or candidates' responsibility and trustworthiness.
- This kind of error-based marking does not take into account positive aspects of students' work, which are implicitly grouped together as "non-errors", usually with no impact on grades.
- The difficulty of the particular task may make it impossible for individual students to show what they have actually learned: the assumption is that if they cannot do X, equally they cannot do Y or Z.
- Criteria for grading and ultimately passing and failing are often not transparent, and certainly not uniform.
- Translations for exams are often unaccompanied by even a minimum contextualization of the task at hand in the form of a translation brief.

Alongside all of these absolutely appropriate criticisms, we find the essential criticism of this kind of testing: it is unaligned with the objectives or intended outcomes of the module. Let us turn now to some basic principles of assessment and attempt to apply them to translator training.

> Compare the criticisms above with those you wrote of your own assessment system earlier.

Basic principles for the assessment of learning processes: alignment with outcomes

The assessment of any learning should be linked directly to the objectives or intended outcomes. If we set out to help student attain certain outcomes, then assessment is the instrument we use to check whether they (and we) have succeeded or not, and indeed to generate proposals for solving problems where our programme has not succeeded. You will remember that in Chapter 2 we discussed the importance of formulating intended outcomes so that they are transparent and assessable. This alignment with objectives or outcomes requires much thought to be put into assessment criteria and methods at the design stage of our curricular and syllabus planning, as an essential element of teaching and learning.

Traditionally, assessment is taken to mark the end of the learning process. The teacher sets a task, usually in examination conditions, which s/he then marks in order to be able to decide whether or not the students have reached the level required to pass the module, accumulate credit, proceed to the following level, or receive their diploma. This kind of assessment involving a grade, or an accreditation, is known as summative assessment. In more-student centred approaches, a more central role is assigned to the other major form of assessment in the learning process. Formative assessment is any marking, correction or comment which gives students feedback on their learning precisely in order to help them learn more, or better. The two functions are not mutually exclusive, in that even final examinations used for summative assessment may have a formative role if marked and returned to students with comments (written or oral) on how to improve. It is important not to confuse formative assessment with continuous assessment, the aim of which is often essentially summative (to provide a series of grades leading to a final mark), although of course a series of frequent small-scale tasks which are corrected will provide feedback to students for further learning.

Another important form of assessment is initial diagnosis or needs analysis. This was dealt with in Chapter 3, so let us simply remember that designing instruments to diagnose the students' starting point for any module, unit or course is an important skill for any teacher, which will help to ensure that teaching and learning activities are pertinent in nature and level.

If assessment is to measure the achievement of intended learning outcomes, let us return precisely to those outcomes in order to discuss how this may best be done. Let us take one of the overall aims we put forward in Chapter 2.

- A teaching unit midway through an introductory module to translation: *By the end of this unit, students will be able to identify documentary sources other than dictionaries of use to the translator, understand how to use them efficiently, and evaluate their accessibility and reliability in different translation situations.*

This outcome is formulated at the lowest or most specific level, an individual teaching unit. Let us analyse step by step the different aspects which we may take into account in our unit design.

Firstly, do we actually need to assess each individual unit? The answer is usually yes, in that each unit contributes to the overall aim of the module and in turn to that of the course or programme. This does not mean that we actually need a mark for each unit, but that each student should know to what extent they have achieved the specific objective, and the teacher should be aware of how the class as a whole has advanced, and where problems may persist in order to take remedial action.

Does this mean that we need to do a series of mini-examinations? Certainly not! There is a wide range of instruments at our disposal for gauging to what degree students have learned what is intended.

What kind of assessment are we talking about here? This is formative assessment, in that the intention is to consolidate and contribute to learning. The idea is not to obtain marks, although there is of course nothing to prevent us from keeping a record of performance which may then have some sort of impact on the final grade we are obliged to register.

Can we assess this particular outcome by asking students to carry out a translation task? With difficulty. As we noted above, the problem with translating as a basis for assessing the component parts of translator competence (outcomes), and certainly with a formative function, is that there are simply too many variables in play. Although teachers tend to reach intuitive conclusions on the origins of students' problems or errors, there is little actual evidence to confirm them, particularly if there is no direct communication with the student other than the written translation itself. The specific outcome in our example is better assessed with an instrument designed specifically for that purpose.

Do we need to design teaching and learning activities and then others for assessment? Not necessarily. The teaching and learning activities themselves may also serve for formative and even summative assessment purposes, as long as this is contemplated when they are designed. In any case, both sets of activities should be designed together.

Let us look at some suggestions for formative assessment activities for our example (there are many more!).

- *Individual activity* Students are given a translation commission, with a detailed brief, and asked to identify the elements of the commission for which they would need to use documentary resources. For each of these elements, they are then asked to identify potential resources, to consult them, and then to appraise their accessibility and reliability for the commission under study. This appraisal may be carried out before translating the text, after doing so, or without translating it, although the usefulness and reliability of the different sources may only become clear on actually translating. There is, however, no need to correct the translation as a final product at this point. The questions put to the students may be answered in writing or orally in short interviews or in tutorial sessions; and simultaneously with the activity itself (in class, the library or the computer room) or retrospectively (on completing the activity outside a class session). The answers may be given to the teacher, a tutor (who may be a more senior student, for example) or may be peer assessed or even self-assessed, in these last two cases perhaps with some support in the form of pointers from the teacher at this early stage in training. Students may be asked also to draw general conclusions on the issue of reliability of sources, in order to encourage higher-level analysis.

- *Group activity* The same activity may be carried out in small groups or syndicates such as those described in Chapter 6. In this case, the initial questions put to the students lead to debate within the group, the conclusions of which may then be shared with the plenary, the teacher, a tutor, or another workgroup (peer assessment).

And now a suggestion for incorporating assessment of this outcome into final summative assessment. Remember that final summative assessment should cover all intended outcomes. Let us suppose for this example that the method chosen is an individual translation project or even an examination.

- One or several short questions, covering different intended outcomes, accompany an actual translation task with a specific brief. A possible formulation for the outcome taken as our example might be:
  Identify appropriate documentary resources for solving X (where X is any translation problem covered by the syllabus and present in the commission to be assessed). Which do you consider to be most reliable? Justify your answer.
  Notice that this kind of short question-and-answer exercise alongside an actual translation may be oral or written, and allows the assessor to understand each student's individual translation process much better than the translation product alone. Our view of student performance is more complete, and allows us to address our set of course objectives in a more reliable way.
- Similarly, students may be required to hand in a complete bibliography of resources used, with comments on usefulness, accessibility, reliability and so on. This is a useful and thought-provoking activity for translation projects, but is less appropriate for examination situations, except when the text type and other information are announced to students beforehand.

> Now take the outcome formulated below relating to the interpersonal
> area of competence for a whole three- or four-year professional transla-
> tor training programme) and think of possible assessment activities, firstly
> for formative assessment throughout different course modules, and sec-
> ondly for summative purposes in an end-of- programme final assessment
> to obtain the corresponding diploma.
>
> *Students will be able to justify to others the decisions they have taken*
> *during translation, appraise those of others involved in the process and*
> *communicate their opinions in such a way as to avoid or resolve poten-*
> *tial conflict.*

Making translation exams more realistic

Traditional translation examinations are criticized from different points of view
at the beginning of this chapter. On the whole, it is preferable for formative
assessment to take place throughout a module and for the summative assessment to be based on several and varied tasks or activities carried out at different
points in the module and taking into account the level of progress which can
reasonably be required at each. These tasks or activities may be set by the teacher,
agreed with students, or even chosen entirely by them (see the section on portfolios below). It is, however, the case that in many systems final examinations
are compulsory, whether for all students or only for those not passing continuous assessment, for example; whether they constitute all or part of the final
summative grade awarded. Systems combining continuous assessment worth a
percentage of the final grade with final exams, or offering final exams as a
second chance to those who do not quite attain the intended level in continuous
assessment, are frequent. In this case, in some circumstances teachers will be
able to replace traditional final examinations with other final assessment tasks
such as take-home translation commissions, to be completed in a short period
of time (24 or 48 hours, for instance). In other institutions, this will not be possible, and students will necessarily have to carry out a series of activities and
tasks in "examination conditions". If we find ourselves in this situation, how
can we improve the conditions and make them more realistic and more conducive to students actually demonstrating learning, which is after all the aim of the
exercise?

> What do your institution's regulations stipulate regarding final assess-
> ment and examinations? Is it possible for you exclusively to use continuous

> assessment to establish a final grade? What is the relation between con-
> tinuous and final assessment?
>
> If you must set final examinations, write some suggestions as to how to
> improve on the traditional model ("Translate this text into X, with(out) a
> dictionary, in a maximum period of 2 hours").

Now consider the following ideas, drawn from different authors and colleagues'
practice and experience (see further reading).

* Translation examinations do not necessarily have to consist (only) of translations. Students may be asked to carry out pre-translation tasks and
  comment on them, to analyse translations and to comment on their own
  translations, as well as or instead of actually submitting a target text.
  Which activities are appropriate will depend on the outcome(s) we are
  assessing.
* Resources permitted for use in examinations should also depend on the
  outcomes being assessed, and should normally not be limited only to
  dictionaries. The availability of resources for translation tasks should reflect professional practice as closely as possible, which will normally
  involve access to computers and to the Internet. Note I say "normally",
  as each assessment activity will be designed to assess a specific outcome,
  for which different resources will be needed or not.
* Tasks may be made more realistic by eliminating the element of surprise
  which we teachers are often over-fond of at examination time! Professional translators rarely find themselves in situations in which they have
  to translate totally unknown texts in a short period of time without any
  form of preparation; this is a particularly important criticism if documentary resources are not available in the examination room and students
  have to rely on those they themselves can take. The element of surprise
  (which adds further stress to an already stressful situation) can be elimi-
  nated or reduced in different ways. The examination text may be made
  available some time before the actual examination and students allotted
  time to carry out documentary research (in a library, a computer room)
  before the examination itself begins. These activities may then be commented on and also assessed, as an integral part of the translation process.
  Teachers may announce text type, subject area and content keywords
  allowing preparation of parallel texts and terminology prior to the examination (Sánchez 2004). Again, this allows assessment of these tasks.
* Timing is important: teachers should ensure that the texts chosen for this

kind of test can realistically be translated and other activities completed in the time allotted.

- A clear translation brief allowing students to contextualize the task at hand should always accompany the source text; instructions as to presentation and type of translation required (final version for publication or revision, summary, etc.) should be extremely clear.
- Students should be amply aware of assessment and grading criteria (see below). If we are assessing specific outcomes, our criteria should be based on these, and not on an overall assessment of the quality of the translation produced (unless this is the outcome we are explicitly assessing, at the end of a programme, for example).

An alternative method: the translation portfolio

In assessment based on portfolios, it is the students, not the teacher, who decide what kind of evidence best reflects their learning. A portfolio is a collection of items which demonstrate, in the individual student's view, the learning which has actually taken place. The items must, then, be related to the intended outcomes of the module or programme. As students in general are not used to this kind of freedom or responsibility, care must be taken to ensure that they understand the nature of the collection of items they are to hand in, and in particular that they understand how much is expected of them. There may be a tendency to submit too much work. Some class time may be devoted to reaching agreement on a rough composition of the portfolio, an interesting exercise in itself as a brainstorming or set of buzz group activities may produce a wealth of interesting and innovative proposals for kinds of evidence of acquiring translator competence. These ideas may then be presented and debated in the plenary group and a "contract" reached describing the portfolio in approximate terms; approximate in order not to exclude innovative and creative choices of evidence.

List some examples of evidence you think might be appropriate for a learning portfolio submitted at the end of a final year specialized translation module in your language combination.

Have you included any items which are not sample translations? Notice that if you have some difficulty thinking of items, then students may have much more. Careful preparation is necessary for this kind of student-centred assessment to work well.

The following is a possible structure for a translation portfolio:

- An introduction in which the student explains clearly the objectives of the portfolio and its structure.
- The items themselves. How many there should be will vary. Biggs (2003) suggests a maximum of 4, although clearly this will depend on the nature of the items, on the class "contract" and so on. Agreed conditions of the kind "of the four items, a minimum of one and maximum of three items should be translations done by the student", or "sample translations should be between 500 and 1000 words long" may be useful.
- For each individual item an explanation of its value in the portfolio, why it has been chosen and what learning it demonstrates. Some form of overall self-assessment statement may also be included.

Suggestions of items might be:

- Sample translations (format, length, subject area and so on depending on the module)
- Commentaries on translations (usually, but not necessarily the student's own)
- Revision work carried out by the student (usually with comment)
- Glossaries drawn up by the student (usually with comment)
- Review of a book from the module's bibliography, perhaps covering the type of translation involved in the module from a theoretical point of view
- Assessment of one of the student's translations by an expert in the subject area, or by a professional translation agency; peer assessment may also by used here
- A small piece of market research, or customer/user survey for the kind of translation involved (asking medical researchers how they usually work with their translators, for example)
- An analysis of how elements such as exchange programmes or work placements have contributed to learning applicable to the module being assessed...

Grading of portfolio work is usually conducted on a holistic basis, using explicit criteria of the kind described in the following section.

Grading: norm referencing versus criterion referencing

We mention above that, traditionally, grading (of translations, as the single most frequent kind of exercise) has taken as a reference point a notional "perfect" translation (10/10, 20/20, 100%...), with points deducted for each error found by the teacher. Occasionally, plus points are awarded for particularly good solutions. As with the traditional form of examining, criticism made be made of this way of grading from several points of view:

*   It is the translation as a product which is being evaluated, not student learning
*   The concept of the perfect translation, however implicit, sits uncomfortably with any modern view of translation activity
*   Emphasis is on what students do wrong, not what they have learned
*   Calculating the exact value of a particular error is an immensely complicated task, and can easily end up being arbitrary, hard to justify and far from transparent
*   Seemingly objective numerical values are in essence extremely subjective as the consideration of each individual error involves a large degree of subjective evaluation and decision-making.

Consider the following questions relating to grading, and justify your answer in each case:

❑   How serious do you consider a spelling mistake in the students' native language to be?
❑   Do you penalize late submission of translation work? How?
❑   How do you evaluate blank spaces left in a translation done under examination conditions (where the use of documentary resources brought by the student, but no others, is allowed)?
❑   Some 30% of the class group have not completed the translation set for an examination. Do you penalize them for this?
❑   A key term in a scientific translation is mistranslated throughout the text in a piece of work done outside class and submitted for assessment. All other aspects of this student's translation are excellent. How do you take this into account in the grade?

If you compare your answers to these questions with other colleagues', you will probably find a wide diversity of opinions on each of these points, leading us back to the conclusion that there is little consensus on translation assessment and certainly nothing intrinsically objective about grading decisions.

An important dichotomy in grading practice is that between norm-referenced and criterion-referenced assessment. Norm-referenced assessment is the grading practice which establishes "typical", or even compulsory, statistical distributions of grades, of the kind A = the top 10%, B = the following 25%, C = the following 30%, D = the following 25%, and E = the bottom 10%.

The kind of approach (used, surprisingly, in working documents for the European Higher Education Area) means that students' performance is measured in comparative or competitive terms, not in terms of individual learning. This approach is difficult to justify in student-centred terms, as it actually predetermines that some students will not perform well. While it may be the case that some students may not do well, surely our greatest challenge as teachers is for those who find learning more difficult (or less interesting) actually to perform better! Student-centred approaches will therefore favour what is called criterion-referenced assessment, where grading is directly dependent on learning and is based on the degree of attainment of the intended outcomes which form the basis of the entire teaching and learning process.

In criterion-referenced assessment, criteria should be transparent and should be discussed with students. Normally, basic attainment of the intended outcomes will mark the "pass/fail" divide, and higher-levels of learning and attainment will win upper grades. Although essentially qualitative in nature and normally expressed in letters or in descriptive terms, grades may be expressed in figures where the system requires. Let us look at an example of criteria for this kind of approach.

Context: introductory module on professional translation practice
Intended outcome: Students will be able to identify translation problems arising from cultural difference between source and target readership, and to propose appropriate solutions for these problems.
Student assessment activity: A short (150-200 word) translation with a clear brief in which there are several problems arising from cultural difference. Students carry out the translation and then give a brief comment on the cultural problems they have found and the solutions they propose.
Assessment procedures: The teacher has selected the text to be translated on the basis of the cultural difficulties it poses for the translator, which should be relatively accessible for trainees at this stage. A combination of the student's actual translation (where the solutions can be seen), and the comment (where it is easier to see whether the problems have been identified, and to follow each student's translation process) make it relatively simple to establish whether or not each student has attained this intended outcome.
Criteria for grading:

A   Excellent. The student has identified all the cultural differences and has proposed appropriate solutions in all or almost all cases.
B   Very good. The student has identified almost all the cultural differences and in most cases has been able to propose appropriate solutions.
C   Good. The student has identified most cultural differences between the two readerships, and has been able to propose appropriate solutions in a significant number of cases.

D   Satisfactory. The student has identified a significant number of cultural
        differences between the two readerships, and has been able on occasion
        to propose appropriate solutions.

E   Unsatisfactory. The student has not identified a significant number of
        cultural differences between the two readerships, and where these have
        been identified they are not dealt with in an appropriate fashion within
        the translation brief

Now design an assessment activity for the following specific intended
outcome, and write grading criteria for it:
Context: introductory module on scientific translation
Intended outcome: Students will be able to find appropriate terminology
and use it in a coherent and appropriate fashion.
Student assessment activity: ....
Assessment procedures: ....
Criteria for grading: ....

The grades awarded for different aspects, each related to outcomes, may be
collated on a form of the kind proposed below in Figure 14, and a final grade
reached on the basis of the student's overall performance. Some teachers will
prefer to convert qualitative grades to quantitative for ease of calculation, although care should be taken when grades are from different stages of a module
to take student progress into account: higher grades at the end of the module
should normally be taken to indicate that learning has taken place, allowing
lower earlier grades to be discarded or given much less weighting.

Who assesses?

Traditionally, it is the teacher or some form of examination board who is responsible for carrying out assessment. In many systems, regulations will establish
who may or must award and confirm final grades; in others regulations are much
more flexible. In most cases there is some room for leeway, particularly for
formative assessment activities, and for continuous summative assessment. Some
of the alternatives to traditional assessment by the teacher are peer assessment,
self assessment and assessment by external experts.

   Peer assessment is that which is carried out by other students from the same
group or level. Comment from peers may be better received than from teachers.
It offers the opportunity not only for students to receive feedback from fellow
students, but also in turn to give their own comments on other students' work.
Apart from the benefit derived by the student (or small group) whose work is

being assessed, all students benefit by developing the ability to evaluate, to justify decisions and comment, and to revise translations.

Self assessment is that carried out by the students themselves of their own work and progress. Self-monitoring is a crucial skill in general in any profession; in translation it is perhaps most important for those who are to become free-lance translators, but is in general recognised as an important component of translation competence or expertise. It is also a difficult skill to acquire, and many teachers find that it is better to introduce self-assessment after students become accustomed to carrying out peer assessment. Self-assessment can be made easier if short questionnaires or scripts encouraging reflection are provided by the teacher:

- *What particular difficulties have you come up against in doing this translation?*
- *How have you gone about solving them?*
- *Are you satisfied with the solutions you have found?*
- *If not, what else could you have done (and what has prevented you from doing so)?*

The answers to these may be given, in writing or orally, to the teacher, serving as the basis for regular review meetings with individual students; they may be taken to work group meetings where fellow students propose solutions to their classmates' problems; they may simply serve as a record of their progress for the students themselves. A colleague at my institution asks each student to identify their own particular "Achilles' heel" (recurring problem/s or weakness/es), and to design a work plan to eliminate it/them, in a fairly elaborate formative self-assessment system (Way, forthcoming). Note that this kind of instrument can prove especially useful in distance learning situations.

In some university systems, the figure of external examiner exists to ensure homogeneity of standards across institutions. In interpreter training, it is frequent to find representatives of the conference interpreting profession on final examination boards. Here, by external assessment, however, I am not referring to this kind of external participation in summative assessment, but rather to bringing in professional translators from outside the training institution to give occasional feedback on student translations and other tasks. It is important for these evaluators to be made aware of the formative function of this kind of exercise, as they may tend to be over-demanding at times. It is, nonetheless, positive for trainees to come into contact with professional criteria for quality assessment, and to be able to contrast them with those applied in the academic context, and indeed to question both! Used at appropriate (usually advanced) points in training and for well-chosen tasks, this kind of assessment can prove to be highly motivating.

A variation on this kind of assessment is "user" assessment, that is assessment by real potential readers of a particular target text: a doctor for a medical text, a solicitor for a legal text, a tourist for an information leaflet... These real readers may be asked for oral or written feedback, or may be invited to a classroom session where translations are being discussed. Or students may be required to find their own real reader, ask for a written report, which they then submit with the translation.

Whoever carries out the assessment, feedback in the form of reports can be simplified by the use of a form listing aspects to be assessed (based on intended outcomes) and offering evaluation on a four- or five-point scale (1-5, A-E, etc.), reflecting explicit grading criteria.

Aspect of text being assessed	A	B	C	D	E
Use of specialised terminology					
Readability					
...					

Figure 14. Outline of assessment report form

Prepare an assessment report form for a teaching and learning activity you have designed for one of the teaching units on your module. Use the intended outcomes of the unit as a starting point for the list of aspects to be assessed. Who will fill in this report form: the individual student, a work group collectively, another student, another work group, an external, you? Justify your choice of evaluator.

Individual versus group assessment

In chapter 6, we mentioned briefly that one of the difficulties associated with group work is assessment. Teachers and students are reticent about giving the same grade to all members of a team, as all those involved are aware that there are often differences between individuals in input, effort and learning. Yet, if all or most course work is carried out in teams, summative assessment based on individual activities or tasks is unfair. This difficulty is recognised in most literature on collaborative learning, where the following proposals, as alternatives to simply giving each member the same collective grade, may be found (see for example Gibbs 1995):

• Require individual members of each group to submit a diary or log in which they register and comment on their participation in team work. This log may constitute an element to be assessed in the final grade awarded to each student, thus modulating the collective grade.

- Ask work groups to submit a collective report on the functioning of the team, how work was shared out, problems encountered and so on, in which they evaluate in quantitative or qualitative terms the relative contribution of each member to the task; this report should be the result of debate and consensus amongst members, and may constitute the basis on which the teacher awards individual grades, or simply allow more in-depth assessment of the process.

- Give each group a numerical grade multiplied by the number of members (e.g. 55% x 4 members = 220 points), and allow them to share out the points (perhaps within certain limits, such as a maximum 15% difference between the highest and the lowest grade, or excluding fail grades for individuals if the group grade is a pass). The result should be communicated officially in writing to the teacher, and may (should) be accompanied by a justification.

Any measure of this kind should be notified to students before work is carried out, and indeed debated with them at a plenary session, where specific rules may be laid down for the entire module.

Analyse the ideas given above for the sharing out of team work grades. If you were to apply them in your modules, what difficulties would you foresee? How do they fit in with a criterion-referenced approach to assessment?

Can you suggest alternative approaches to the assessment of team work?

Programme evaluation

One final kind of evaluation or assessment is that carried out of the teaching and learning process as a whole. Just as students need constant feedback in order to help them learn, teachers and programmes need constant feedback in order to help them improve. In most institutions and indeed companies, there is some form of quality assessment, and in many of quality enhancement, that is a system designed to identify where improvement may be made and actually to foment that improvement taking place. This is not the place to enter into a detailed description or discussion of these systems, although it is important briefly to mention them and to go into a little detail of how individual teachers can implement their own quality enhancement processes in their teaching. Course or programme assessment by all those involved (teachers, students, administrative staff, authorities and other stakeholders such as future employers) is an essential part of all course design and a key factor in achieving and maintaining high levels of quality in teaching and learning.

> What kind of teaching assessment exists in your institution: student questionnaires, peer assessment, a central unit responsible for evaluating teaching and helping to improve? What consequences does the assessment have (is it formative or summative?): promotion, salary incentives, contract renewal, further training? What is your opinion of this system?

Irrespective of institutional systems, individual teachers may implement their own formative assessment techniques in order to have feedback from students and colleagues from which to learn and introduce improvements. One of the most commonly used techniques is that of the student questionnaire, which is possibly the most reliable way of knowing student opinion, as others (debates, interviews and so on) may be very useful, but uncomfortable for those involved. These questionnaires should not be too long, should not ask questions students cannot answer, and (where the intention is overall assessment of a module) should normally be applied after assessment has been completed and the results published, as this takes away part of the pressure to "please" the teacher, and also allows evaluation of the entire teaching and learning process, including summative assessment. Items should be clearly formulated, unambiguously, directly related to the module in question, and leave some room for additional comments ("open" questions), which often give unexpected and interesting results. In some institutions, help may be available on how to design simple and effective instruments of this kind.

> Think carefully about different items you might include in a questionnaire for students for one of the modules you teach, and what you can learn from each one of them. Try to write the questionnaire itself (maximum 20 questions or items). Then decide how you would administer the questionnaire (format, time, reception), foreseeing possible difficulties, and planning solutions for them.

Self assessment is, of course, important for all teachers and may take many individual forms. For example, some teachers keep a diary of their teaching where they note down what has worked well and what has not, with some ideas as to why and how to improve. Others prefer to carry out an overall analysis of their teaching at the end of each unit or each module, eliminating material and activities which have not given the desired results, and planning new material and activities for future editions well in advance. In some institutional settings, teaching portfolios are required for staff selection and promotion procedures, offering teachers a valuable opportunity to present their own assessment of their teaching by collecting and collating evidence of good practice.

> Think of items you might include in a teaching portfolio. In what way does each of them offer evidence of good teaching? Actually collating this kind of evidence is a valuable exercise in self-assessment even where it is not a requirement or standard practice in your institutional setting. And you never know when it may come in useful for external purposes!

Peer assessment is probably an under-used instrument in assessing teaching, as many teachers find the situation uncomfortable. For this reason, informal mutual assessment with a close colleague, a "critical friend", may be the best way to start (where institution-wide systems are not already in place). Colleagues attend one or two sessions of each other's classes and then talk over all aspects informally, exchanging ideas, opinions and suggestions for change or improvement in an unthreatening atmosphere. Having tried this kind of assessment, formal peer assessment by an unknown colleague, or assessment by a superior or a committee will be much less traumatic! Lacking this possibility, simply meeting with colleagues to talk about teaching offers positive input and avoids the feeling of isolation some teachers experience.

> What kind of peer assessment could you envisage in your professional situation? How do you feel about this sort of activity? Do you find it threatening in any way? Try to analyse why.

This chapter has covered the major kinds of assessment, except initial needs analysis, dealt with in Chapter 3. The major point made is that assessment should always be directly linked to and depend on intended outcomes. Issues relating to examinations, grading and the evaluation of teaching have also been discussed. With this chapter, the entire curricular design process has now been covered. The last chapter, on training the trainers, aims to underline the importance of trainer training, focusing mainly on courses and materials currently available, and offers a brief conclusion to all the reflections put forward in this book on training translators.

Further reading on the evaluation of translations

The following are only some of the TS publications on translation quality, or which mention it in a wider context.

Gouadec, Daniel (1989) 'Comprendre, évaluer, prévenir. Pratique, enseignement et recherche face à l'erreur et à la faute en traduction'. *TTR* II.2. 35-54.

Hatim, Basil and Ian Mason (1997) *The Translator as Communicator*. London: Routledge.

House, Juliane (1997) *Translation Quality Assessment: A Model Revisited*. Tübingen: Narr.

Klaudy, Kinga. (1995) 'Quality Assessment in School vs Professional Translation'. In Cay Dollerup and Vibeke Appel (eds.) *Teaching Translation and Interpreting 3. New Horizons*. Amsterdam: John Benjamins. 197-206.

Maier, Carol (ed.) (2000) *Evaluation and Translation*. Special issue of *The Translator*. Vol. 6 N°.2.

McAlester, Gerard (2000) 'The Time Factor: a practical evaluation criterion'. In Meta Grosman *et al.* (eds.) *Translation into Non-Mother Tongues – In Professional Practice and Training*. Tübingen: Stauffenburg. 133-140.

Nord, Christiane (1996) 'El error en traducción: categorías y evaluación'. In Amparo Hurtado Albir (ed.) *La enseñanza de la traducción*. Castellón: Universitat Jaume I. 91-108.

Pym, Anthony (1992) 'Translation Error Analysis and the Interface with Language Teaching'. In Cay Dollerup and Anne Loddegaard (eds.) *Teaching Translation and Interpreting. Training, Talent, and Experience*. Amsterdam: John Benjamins. 279-90.

Sager, Juan (1989) 'Quality and Standards – the evaluation of translations'. In Catriona Picken (ed.) *The Translator's Handbook*. 2ª ed. London: Aslib. 91-102.

Waddington, Christopher (1999) *Estudio comparativo de diferentes métodos de evaluación de traducción general (inglés-español)*. Madrid: Universidad Pontificia Comillas de Madrid.

Further reading on professional standards

The following are some of the major standards used by the profession:

The DIN 2345 Standard, Deutsche Institut für Normung.

The LISA QA Model, Localization Industry Standards Association (LISA). See http://www.lisa.org

European Committee for Standardization (CEN) European Quality Standard for Translation Services EN-15038. For comment on this forthcoming standard by a member of the working committee responsible for it, see Juan José Arevalillo Doval (2005) Quality Standard for Translation Services: What's behind it? At http://www.lisa.org/globalizationinsider/2005/04/la_norma-europe.html

Languages National Training Organization (LNTO) (2001) *The National Standards in Translating*. London: LNTO.

Further reading on assessing student learning

Biggs, John (2003) *Teaching for Quality Learning at University. What the Student Does*. Maidenhead: Open University Press [2nd edition: Chapters 8 and 9 "Assessing for learning quality I: principles" and "Assessing for learning quality I: practice".

Gosling, David and Jenny Moon (2001) *How to Use Learning Outcomes and Assessment Criteria*. London: Southern England Consortium for Credit Accumulation and Transfer (SEEC).

Wakeford, Richard (2003) 'Principles of Student Assessment'. In Heather Fry, Steve Ketteridge and Stephanie Marshall (eds.) *A Handbook for Teaching and Learning in Higher Education. Enhancing Academic Practice*. London: RoutledgeFalmer. 42-61

Further reading on course evaluation

European Association for Quality Assurance in Higher Education: http://www.enqa.net

International Network for Quality Assurance Agencies in Higher Education: http://www.inqaahe.org

For a critical appraisal of different approaches to quality in higher education: Chapter 13 "The Reflective Institution: quality assurance through quality enhancement" in Biggs, John (2003) *Teaching for Quality Learning at University. What the Student Does*. Maidenhead: Open University Press [2nd edition].

9. Training the Trainers

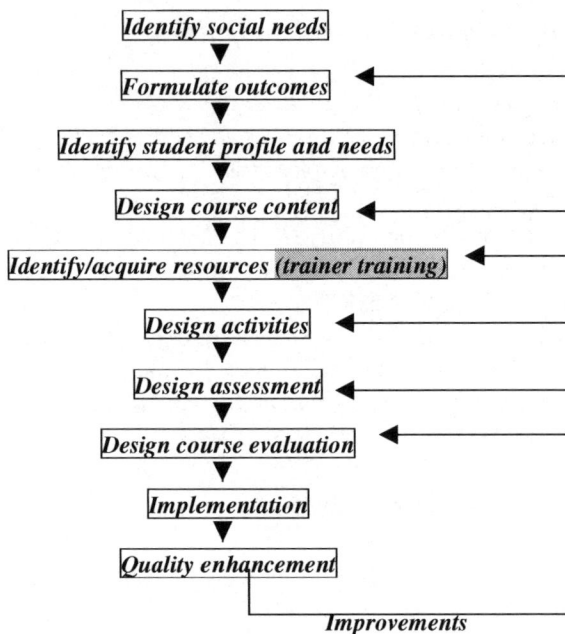

| Identify social needs |
| Formulate outcomes |
| Identify student profile and needs |
| Design course content |
| Identify/acquire resources (trainer training) |
| Design activities |
| Design assessment |
| Design course evaluation |
| Implementation |
| Quality enhancement |

Improvements

Summary and aims

This final chapter aims to offer a brief overview of the possibilities open to those requiring training as trainers. There is no doubt that there is a need for translator trainer training, and similarly that there is little of it available. The chapter will offer some suggestions for action in this field, with a brief outline of how to approach the design of training programmes, and offer information on existing resources for trainer training. By the end of the chapter, readers should be able to decide whether existing resources are appropriate for them and, if not, to design an action plan to cover their own current training needs.

Need for trainer training and trainer competence

It will have become clear by now that in my opinion translator trainers require training in order to carry out their task as educators efficiently. In Chapter 3 the question of who should train translators is discussed in some detail, and my essential conclusion is that those who do so should first and foremost be competent trainers. The different areas of competence or expertise required in order to be a competent translator trainer are:

* Professional translation practice
* Translation Studies as an academic discipline
* Teaching skills

Although the first two are essential for overall translator trainer competence, they are a little like the language competence one expects of a professional translator, in that they constitute prerequisites rather than the central competence we are interested in. In this book we are specifically interested in the last of the three, which we could subdivide into at least the following "subcompetences" or areas of competence:

* *Organizational:*
    o the ability to design courses and appropriate teaching and learning activities
    o the ability to apply and manage these
    o the ability to design, apply and manage appropriate assessment activities
* *Interpersonal:*
    o the ability to work collaboratively with trainees towards their learning goals
    o the ability to work in a training team
    o the ability to act as a mentor for trainees
* *Instructional:*
    o the ability to present content and explain clearly
    o the ability to stimulate discussion and reflective thinking
    o the ability to arouse interest and enthusiasm
* *Contextual or professional:*
    o understanding of the educational context in which training takes place (local, national, international)
    o understanding of the teaching profession
* *Instrumental:*
    o knowledge of training resources of all kinds and ability to apply them appropriately and usefully to the training process

Most, if not all, of these aspects have been covered to some extent in the previous chapters.

Designing trainer training

If we follow our own recommendations for the design of training courses the first step will be to establish learning outcomes, taking into the account social or market needs. New or existing translator training courses clearly generate a need for specialized trainers, a need rarely attended by specific institutional training programmes. It is perhaps fair to say that the first two major areas of competence, in professional translation and in Translation Studies as an academic discipline, are sufficiently catered for by existing undergraduate and postgraduate courses. It is the third major area, that of actual teaching competence, which is to be found lacking. Following again our own approach, careful attention needs to be paid to institutional and local context. Despite the internationalization of higher education and the globalization of the translation profession, there continue to be important local constraints on training and trainers. These should be taken into account also in trainer training. Research into teacher training in general has suggested that the closer to the trainer's actual context, the better. This would tend to suggest that specific local (perhaps departmental) programmes may be the best way to guarantee learning, which is not to say that external participation is not to be encouraged!

As to learning outcomes, an initial approximate formulation of these may be derived, taking into account the local context, from the tentative listing of teaching competences above, just as we did with translator competence in Chapter 2.

> Write intended outcomes for translator trainer training in your context based on the description of trainer competence above. Remember the indications regarding the formulation of outcomes given in Chapter 2.

> Let us give some brief consideration to the participants in this training process. Write a short description of the learners' profile on undertaking such a programme. Take into account issues such as prior knowledge and motivation. Now describe the teachers' profile. Are suitable trainers available in your context? (See Chapter 3.)

This brings us to the design of teaching and learning activities for training. Some examples of these may be found in the different activities included in shaded boxes throughout this book, although of course there are many more possibilities. Particular attention could be paid to actual teaching practice with input from colleagues (peer teaching and assessment), and to team work. Many of the activities suggested in the different chapters of this book, for example, will produce much richer results if carried out in small groups or teams.

> Take one of the intended outcomes you have written for trainer training, and design at least one related learning activity. Which resources do you

> need in order to carry out the activity? Are they readily available in your context?

And finally, to assessment. There is little doubt that self and peer assessment are key elements in trainer training, and that although summative assessment may have a role in some systems (for promotion, tenure or contract renewal), it is formative assessment designed to improve actual teaching practice that is of greatest interest to trainers and trainees alike.

Existing resources

There is a variety of resources available to those who already have translation and Translation Studies competence and wish to become translator trainers, or those who already work as translator trainers but wish to improve their training skills. The following is a brief summary; URLs where you can find further information are offered at the end of the chapter under "further reading".

Literature
There is now fairly extensive literature available on translator training, some of which is reviewed in Chapter 1 and more of which is quoted at different points in this book or listed in the bibliography. Further suggestions for finding publications in this field are: *Conference proceedings.* As well as those conferences which are organized specifically on translator training (see for example the series of conferences launched by Cay Dollerup of the University of Copenhagen in 1991, the proceedings of which are listed under further reading), many TS conferences have a section on training, and the published proceedings offer a magnificent range of different approaches to various aspects of training.
TS associations. As mentioned earlier, some academic associations, such as IATIS or EST, have training committees which offer resources such as bibliographies and book reviews in the field of translator training. At the time of writing, the chair of the IATIS Training Committee is working on the initial draft of what promises to be the most complete bibliography to date on the subject.
TS bibliographical data bases. Bibliographical data bases in TS, such as St Jerome's *Translation Studies Abstracts* and *Translation Studies Bibliography* offer detailed and up-to-date information on recent publications in different areas including translator training.
TS journals. Many of the leading journals in TS devote regular space to training issues, course profiles and so on.

Courses
At a *general* level, higher education institutions are increasingly offering

induction courses for new members of the teaching staff, and continuing training courses for existing staff, all of which are of course applicable to many
aspects of translator training.

Specific courses are organized on a regular basis by several universities and
consortia. Of particular interest are the Consortium for Training Translation
Teachers (CTTT) annual one-week seminars in Rennes (France), under the direction of Daniel Gouadec, and at other European locations, under the direction
of Anthony Pym; the Universitat de Vic (Spain) has been running an Annual
Certificate in Collaborative Translation Teaching since 2004, and the University of Monterey (California, USA) held a one-off seminar in 2002. Some
postgraduate and doctoral programmes also offer specific courses or modules
on translator training, as they understand that many of those undertaking postgraduate research into translation are likely to take up teaching posts and thus
be involved in translator training. It would be impossible for a book of this kind
to offer full information on all of these, particularly as courses change frequently.

> Think of your own situation, and note the resources you have available at
> your own institution and which may be of use to you.
>
> Now think of your departmental situation and note down the main areas
> where you think training might be useful for staff. Design a short train-
> ing course to attend those needs, taking into account intended outcomes,
> participants (teachers and learners), resources and assessment (where
> necessary).

Concluding remarks

Writing these pages has offered me a very rewarding opportunity to re-read
what so many experienced translator trainers have had to say about their teaching, and to revise in depth my own teaching practice. Discussions with close
colleagues in Granada and at other training institutions during this reading, reflecting and writing process have proved to be enormously interesting, enriching
and indeed challenging. I have also had occasion to debate many of the points
covered here with undergraduate and postgraduate students I am currently working with. In this way, writing this book has proved to be an immensely rewarding
personal experience, which has led me to new reflections on teaching and learning
in our field. I trust that the reflections put forward here will also be of use to
colleagues, old and new, and particularly that they will serve as a starting point
for analysis of and critical engagement with daily practice in our institutions
and organizations.

This chapter has offered some brief reflections on trainer training, in particular a tentative description of trainer competence, together with some initial ideas on training resources. It is intended to constitute a starting point for further individual or group action to improve teaching practice.

Further reading on teaching in higher education

Biggs, John (2003) *Teaching for Quality Learning at University. What the Student Does.* Maidenhead: Open University Press [2nd edition].

Cannon, Robert and David Newble (2000) *A Handbook for Teachers in Universities and Colleges.* London: Kogan Page.

Cowan, John (1998) *On Becoming an Innovative University Teacher.* Buckingham: Society for Research into Higher Education and Open University.

Fry, Heather; Steve Ketteridge and Stephanie Marshall (eds.) (2003) *A Handbook for Teaching and Learning in Higher Education. Enhancing Academic Practice.* London: RoutledgeFalmer.

Gibbs, Graham, Sue Habeshaw and Trevor Habeshaw (1994) *53 Interesting Ways to Teach: 12 Do-it-yourself Staff Development Exercises.* Bristol: Technical and Educational Services.

Gibbs, Graham and Trevor Habeshaw (1993) *Preparing to Teach: An Introduction to Effective Teaching in Higher Education.* Bristol: Technical and Educational Services.

González, J. and R. Wagenaar (2003) *Tuning Educational Structures in Europe. Final Report. Phase One.* Bilbao: Universidad de Deusto. Also available at: http://www.relint.deusto.es/TuningProject/index.htm

Tight, Malcolm (ed.) (2003) *The RoutledgeFalmer Reader in Higher Education.* London: RoutledgeFalmer.

Further reading on translator trainer training

Please refer also to the general bibliography on translator training at the back of the book.

Information on CTTT activities and other trainer training events is available at: http://isg.urv.es/cttt/cttt/cttt.html

Information on the annual Universitat de Vic seminar is available at http://www.uvic.es/fchtd/especial/en/collaborative_translation_teaching.html

Information on the IATIS Training Committee is available at http://www.iatis.org

The four books of proceedings from the Teaching Translation and Interpreting conferences launched in 1991 by Cay Collerup of the University of Copenhagen are:

Dollerup, Cay and Vibeke Appel (eds.) (1996) *Teaching Translation and Interpreting 3. New Horizons.* Amsterdam: John Benjamins.

Dollerup, Cay and Annette Lindegaard (eds.) (1994) *Teaching Translation and Interpreting 2. Insights, Aims, Visions. Papers from the Second Language*

International Conference, Elsinore, Denmark 4 - 6 June 1993. Amsterdam: John Benjamins.

Dollerup, Cay and Anne Loddegaard (eds.) (1992*) Teaching Translation and Interpreting. Training, Talent and Experience.* Amsterdam: John Benjamins.

Hung, Eva (ed.) (2002) *Teaching Translation and Interpreting 4. Building Bridges.* Amsterdam: John Benjamins.

Glossary

A language

A language in which a translator or interpreter possesses native-like proficiency

Accreditation

Process leading to some form of certification guaranteeing standards, usually for professional activity, such as translating or interpreting

Aim

Overall objective intended by a whole **programme** of study

Assessment criteria

Predetermined criteria according to which student learning may be assessed

Asynchronous

Taking place at different times: a term used frequently in distance learning, where activities may be carried out by different students at different times. See **synchronous**

B language

A acquired language which a translator or interpreter uses actively in professional practice

Bloom's taxonomy

A taxonomy by Benjamin Bloom (1956) in which learning levels are arranged hierarchically; the taxonomy focuses mainly on the cognitive domain (knowledge, understanding, thinking)

Bologna Process

The process by which European university systems are attempting to harmonize and create a **European Higher Education Area**

Brainstorming

Small group activity in which members share their initial thoughts on a subject, designed to promote creativity

Buzz groups

Small group debate lasting usually no more than 5 minutes; results are usually reported back to the whole class group or plenary

C language

A acquired language which a translator or interpreter uses only passively in professional practice

Collaborative learning

Learning processes based on collective effort and interpersonal relations

Competences (generic and specific)

A combination of skills, knowledge, aptitudes and attitudes, and including disposition to learn as well as know-how; generic competences are those to be attained by all people learning at the same stage (e.g. all undergraduates), whereas specific competences are those to be attained only by those specializing in a particular field

Continuing education

Learning which continues throughout one's life after formal education has finished. See **life-long learning**

Course

An overall structure for teaching and learning leading to a named diploma. See **programme**

Criterion-referenced grading

A process whereby student performance is assessed according to predetermined criteria. See **norm-referenced grading**

Cross-over groups

Small groups formed by temporary redistribution of members of other existing **work groups** or **syndicates**, usually to exchange ideas

Curricular or curriculum design

Process whereby overall intended outcomes, programme structure, activities, sequence and assessment are designed. At lower levels (for individual modules) the process is often referred to as syllabus design.

Deep approach (to learning)

Learning which attempts to understand underlying theory and concepts See **surface approach to learning**, and **strategic approach to learning**

Distance teaching and learning

Any teaching and learning process or programme in which teacher and learner are not physically in the same place. See **face-to-face teaching and learning, and off-campus teaching and learning**

European Higher Education Area

The aim of the **Bologna Process**: a European area where all higher education degrees are mutually understandable and accepted for professional purposes, to which end different mechanisms such as a diploma supplement, a common grading system and two-cycle programme structure are to be implemented by the year 2010. The process also intends to foment student-centred teaching and learning

Face-to-face teaching and learning

Any teaching and learning process or programme in which teacher and learner are physically in the same place. See **distance teaching and learning**

Formative assessment

Any assessment activity designed to give learners feedback on their progress and thus enhance learning

In-house training

Initial or continuing training of staff organized and carried out in a company. See **staff development**

Learner-centred teaching and learning

Any teaching or learning process which takes the student or learner as the essential agent

Learning outcomes (general and specific)

The intended results of an teaching and learning process. General outcomes are expressed for overall programmes or in general terms; specific outcomes for lower-level units such as modules or teaching units, or for specific individual aspects of learning. They are expressed in terms of student learning. See **objectives**

Learning portfolio

A form of assessment whereby the student or learner submits a collection of items of evidence of learning. Originally developed in Fine Arts and similar fields, it is now relatively frequent in other disciplines

Learning styles

A term used to describe preferences or tendencies in the way individuals learn

Lecture

One of the most common teaching methods in higher education, although not in TS. Consists essentially of a presentation by a teacher of salient points of syllabus content

Life-long learning

Learning which continues throughout one's life after formal education has finished. See **continuing education**

Mentoring

Follow-up of students' academic progress. Is also applied to other forms of student support in social, psychological, career, medical and personal matters. Also used in professional situations to describe processes whereby senior translators guide novices through the early stages of their professional experience

Mobility programme

A structure based on inter-institutional agreements permitting students and staff to spend mutually recognized usually extended periods of study at another institution

Module

A unit into which teaching and learning is subdivided on an overall programme. A module may be compulsory for all students, or optional

Motivation (extrinsic and intrinsic)

Reasons driving learners to learn: extrinsic motivation comes from external sources (grades, approval from others); intrinsic motivation from internal curiosity or desire to learn

Needs analysis

Initial diagnosis of students' prior knowledge, expectations and motivation,

along with other personal characteristics which may influence their learning (cultural background)

Norm-referenced grading

A process whereby student performance is assessed according to a predetermined distribution of marks; i.e. depending on peer performance. See
criterion-referenced grading

Objectives (general and specific)

Aims of a teaching and learning process expressed in terms of what teachers or the institution want to achieve. General objectives are formulated
for overall programmes or in general terms; specific objectives for lower-
level units such as modules or teaching units, or for specific individual
aspects of teaching. See **learning outcomes**

Off-campus teaching and learning

Any teaching and learning process or programme in which teacher and
learner are not physically in the same place. See **face-to-face teaching
and learning, and distance teaching and learning**

Pair work

Teaching and learning activities carried out in pairs.

Peer assessment

Assessment by fellow learners (peers)

Peer-tutoring

Teaching and learning activities in which students learn from each other

Programme

An overall structure for teaching and learning leading to a named diploma.
See **course**

Programme evaluation

Process whereby the degree to which a programme achieves its stated aims
is assessed, usually by measuring the satisfaction of students, teachers and
other agents involved, together with results such as drop-out rates, graduate employment rates and so on. See **quality enhancement**

Progression

The process whereby a learner advances to higher levels of learning

Quality enhancement

Any activity or process adopted by institutions and/or teachers to improve
the quality of higher education provision and practice.

Role play

Small group work in which each student adopts a role, usually taken from
professional life (translator, reviser, terminologist, client) in order to simulate real-life situations in training

Self assessment

Assessment carried out by learners themselves

Self-concept

Awareness of one's own personal and social role or identity, in this case as a professional translator

Sequencing

The order in which teachers and institutions organize teaching and learning in order to ensure progression

Situational approach

The approach to translator training based on the idea that only real-life professional situations or closely simulated real-life professional situations can lead to meaningful learning as a future translator

Social constructivism

The approach to learning based on the belief that learning is the product of the interaction of multiple perspectives, the result of which is not only individual learning by also the advance of the whole community

SOLO taxonomy

A taxonomy, developed by Biggs and Collis (1982), of learning outcomes (structure of the observed learning outcome), based on a hierarchy of increasing complexity involving five stages: prestructural; unistructural; multistructural; relational, and extended abstract

Staff development

Initial or continuing training of staff organized and carried out in a company. It is the term used normally for continuing education of teaching staff. See **continuing education**

Strategic approach (to learning)

The approach to learning which adapts according to immediate needs (obtaining high grades, for example) See **deep approach to learning**, and **surface approach to learning**

Student presentation

A presentation made by an individual student or small group of students to the whole class group

Summative assessment

Any assessment activity designed to award grades, permit progression to a higher level, or award a diploma

Surface approach (to learning)

Learning which focuses on details and memorizing facts as opposed to attempting to understand underlying theory and concepts. See **deep approach to learning**, and **strategic approach to learning**

Synchronous

Taking place at the same time. See **asynchronous**

Syndicate

Small work group formed either for the purpose of one particular project or activity, or on a more permanent basis. See **work group**

Tandem work

Pair work carried out at a distance by using new technologies

Task-based approach

The approach to translator training (and language learning) based on designing a series of concrete and brief exercises that help to practise specific points leading to an overall aim and a final product. Task-based approaches are based on the gradual and sequenced attainment of highly specified **learning outcomes**

Teacher-centred

Any teaching or learning process which takes the teacher as the central point or protagonist

Teaching and learning activities

Any individual or group, in-class or out-of-class activity designed to help students attain learning outcomes

Teaching styles

A term used to describe preferences or tendencies in the way individual teachers teach and relate to their students and their professional practice

Team or group work

Any activity carried out collectively, in a small group or team. Collective responsibility is an essential element in this teaching and learning technique

Translation/translator competence

The term(s) used in TS to describe the set of knowledge, skills, attitudes and aptitudes which a translator possesses in order to undertake professional activity in the field

Transmissionist tradition

The teaching tradition in which teachers are the source of knowledge which students acquire from them

Unit

Modules are subdivided into individual teaching and learning units which often focus on one or two specific learning outcomes; one of the lowest levels at which teaching and learning is designed and planned

Work group

Small group of students or learners working together either for the purpose of one particular project or activity, or on a more permanent basis. See **syndicate**

Work placements

Short periods of work experience in a real-life professional environment, such as a translation company; these may be remunerated or not; credit-bearing or not, depending on the national university system

References

Alcina, Amparo (forthcoming) 'Translation Technologies: A Description of the Field and the Classification of Tools and Resources'. *Perspectives. Studies in Translatology.*

Arntz, Reiner (1988) 'Steps towards a Translation-oriented Typology of Technical Texts'. *Meta* XXXIII, no. 4. 468-71.

Biggs, John (1987) *Student Approaches to Learning and Studying.* Hawthorn, Victoria: Australian Council for Educational Research.

------ (1993) 'From theory to Practice: a cognitive systems approach'. *Higher Education Research and Development* 12. 73-86.

------ (2003) *Teaching for Quality Learning at University. What the Student Does.* Maidenhead: Open University Press

------ and Kevin F. Collis (1982) *Evaluating the Quality of Learning: The SOLO Taxonomy.* New York: Academic Press.

Bloom, Benjamin (1956) *Taxonomy of Educational Objectives Handbook I: Cognitive domain.* New York: McGraw-Hill.

Brown, George (1978) *Lecturing and Explaining.* London: Methuen.

Calvo, Elisa (2001) *La evaluación diagnóstica para la traducción jurídica. Diseño de un instrumento de medida.* Unpublished postgraduate dissertation. Universidad de Granada, Spain.

------ (forthcoming) *Desarrollo de la concepción académica y profesional durante los estudios de Traducción e Interpretación por parte del estudiantado.* Doctoral dissertation in progress. University of Granada, Spain. [information on both pieces of research available from calvoelisa@gmail.com]

Caminade, Monique and Anthony Pym (1998) 'Translator-training Institutions'. In Mona Baker (ed.) *Routledge Encyclopedia of Translation Studies.* London: Routledge. 280-285.

Campbell, Stuart (1998) *Translation into the Second Language,* London and New York: Longman.

Cannon, Robert and David Newble (2000) *A Handbook for Teachers in Universities and Colleges.* London: Kogan Page.

Carroll, Judith and Janette Ryan (forthcoming) *Teaching International Students.* London: Routledge.

Chesterman, Andrew and Emma Wagner (2002) *Can Theory Help Translators? A Dialogue Between the Ivory Tower and the Wordface.* Manchester: St Jerome.

Colina, Sonia (2003) *Teaching Translation. From Research to the Classroom.* New York, San Francisco: McGraw Hill.

Cowan, John (1998) *On Becoming an Innovative University Teacher.* Buckingham: Society for Research into Higher Education and Open University.

D'Andrea, Vaneeta-Marie (2003) 'Organizing Teaching and Learning: outcomes-based planning'. In Heather Fry, Steve Ketteridge and Stephanie Marshall (eds.) *A Handbook for Teaching and Learning in Higher Education. Enhancing Academic Practice.* London: RoutledgeFalmer. 26-41.

Delisle, Jean (1980) *L'analyse du discours comme méthode de traduction: Initiation à la traduction française de textes pragmatiques anglais, théorie et pratique.* Ottawa: Presses de l'Université d'Ottawa.[English translation of Part I by Patricia Hogan and Monica Creery: (1988) *Translation: An Interpretive Approach.* Ottawa: University of Ottawa Press].

------ (1992) 'Les manuels de traduction: essai de classification'. *TTR* V, no. 1. 17-48.

------ (1993) *La traduction raisonnée. Manuel d'initiation à la traduction professionnelle de l'anglais vers le français.* Ottawa: Université d'Ottawa.

------ (1998) 'Définition, rédaction et utilité des objectifs d'apprentissage en enseignement de la traduction'. In Isabel García Izquierdo and Joan Verdegal (eds.) *Los estudios de traducción: un reto didáctico.* Castellón: Universitat Jaume I. 13-44.

Dollerup, Cay (1997) 'Issues Today, Challenges Tomorrow: Translation and English as the international lingua franca'. In Marian Labrum (ed.) *The Changing Scene in World Languages. ATA Scholarly Monograph Series Volume IX.* Amsterdam: John Benjamins. 65-82.

Dollerup, Cay and Vibeke Appel (eds.) (1996) *Teaching Translation and Interpreting 3. New Horizons.* Amsterdam: John Benjamins.

Dollerup, Cay and Annette Lindegaard (eds.) (1994) *Teaching Translation and Interpreting 2. Insights, Aims, Visions. Papers from the Second Language International Conference, Elsinore, Denmark 4 - 6 June 1993.* Amsterdam: John Benjamins.

Dollerup, Cay and Anne Loddegaard (eds.) (1992*) Teaching Translation and Interpreting. Training, Talent and Experience.* Amsterdam: John Benjamins.

Durieux, Christine (1988) *Fondement didactique de la traduction technique.* Paris: Didier Erudition.

Fleischmann, Eberhard (ed.) (1997) *Translationsdidaktik.* Tubingen: Narr.

Fry, Heather, Steve Ketteridge and Stephanie Marshall (eds.) *A Handbook for Teaching and Learning in Higher Education. Enhancing Academic Practice.* London: RoutledgeFalmer.

Gabr, Moustafa (2001) 'Toward a Model Approach to Translation Curriculum Development'. In *Translation Journal*, Volume 5 N° 2, available at: http://www.accurapid.com/journal/16edu.htm

García Izquierdo, Isabel and Joan Verdegal (eds.) (1998*) Los estudios de traducción: un reto didáctico.* Castellón: Universitat Jaume I.

Gibbs, Graham (1995) *Learning in Teams. A Tutor Guide.* Oxford: Oxford Centre for Staff Development. [There are also companion publications: *A Student Guide* and *A Student Manual.*]

------, Sue Habeshaw and Trevor Habeshaw (1992) *53 Interesting Things To Do in Your Lectures.* Bristol: Technical and Educational Services.

------ (1994) *53 Interesting Ways to Teach: 12 Do-it-yourself Staff Development Exercises.* Bristol: Technical and Educational Services.

------ and Trevor Habeshaw (1993) *Preparing to Teach: An Introduction to Effective Teaching in Higher Education.* Bristol: Technical and Educational Services.

Gile, Daniel (1995*) Basic Concepts and Models for Interpreter and Translator Train-*

ing. Amsterdam: John Benjamins.

González, Julia and Robert Wagenaar (2003) *Tuning Educational Structures in Europe. Final Report. Phase One,* Bilbao: Universidad de Deusto. Also available at: http://www.relint.deusto.es/TuningProject/index.htm

González Davies, María (coord.) (2003) *Secuencias. Tareas para el aprendizaje interactivo de la traducción especializada.* Barcelona: Octaedro-EUB.

------ (2004) *Multiple Voices in the Translation Classroom.* Amsterdam: John Benjamins.

Gosling, David and Jenny Moon (2001) *How to Use Learning Outcomes and Assessment Criteria.* London: Southern England Consortium for Credit Accumulation and Transfer (SEEC).

Gouadec, Daniel (1989) 'Comprendre, évaluer, prévenir. Pratique, enseignement et recherche face à l'erreur et à la faute en traduction'. *TTR* II.2, 35-54.

------ (1994) 'L'assurance qualité en traduction – perspectives professionnelles, implications pédagogiques'. Unpublished plenary address at the I Jornadas Internacionales de Traducción e Interpretación, Universidad de Las Palmas de Gran Canaria.

------ (ed.) (2000) *Formation des traducteurs. Actes du colloque international Rennes 2 24-25 Septembre 1999.* Paris: Maison du Dictionnaire.

------ (2003) 'Position Paper: Notes on Translator Training'. In Anthony Pym, Carmina Fallada, José Ramón Biau and Jill Orenstein (eds.) *Innovation and E-Learning in Translator Training.* Tarragona: Universitat Rovira i Virgili. 11-19. [Also available at http://www.fut.es/~apym/symp/intro.html or in N°. 1 of the journal *Across Languages and Cultures*].

Grellet, Françoise (1991) *Apprendre à traduire. Typologie d'exercices de traduction.* Nancy: Presses Universitaires de Nancy.

Gros Salvat, B. (1995) *Teorías cognitivas de enseñanza y aprendizaje.* Barcelona: EUB.

Grosman, Meta, Mira Kadric, Irena Kovacic and Mary Snell-Hornby (eds.) (2000) *Translation into Non-Mother Tongues in Professional Practice and Training.* Tubingen: Stauffenburg.

Habeshaw, Sue, Graham Gibbs and Trevor Habeshaw (1992) *53 Problems With Large Classes.* Bristol: Technical and Educational Services.

Habeshaw, Sue, Trevor Habeshaw and Graham Gibbs (1992) *53 Interesting Things to do in your Seminars and Tutorials.* Bristol: Technical and Educational Services.

Hansen, Gyde (ed.) (1999) *Probing the Process in Translation: Methods and Results. Copenhagen Studies in Language* 24.

------ (2002) *Empirical Translation Studies. Process and Product. Copenhagen Studies in Language* 27.

Hatim, Basil (2001) *Teaching and Researching Translation.* Harlow: Longman.

------ and Ian Mason. (1997) *The Translator as Communicator.* London: Routledge.

------ and Jeremy Munday (2004) *Translation. An Advanced Resource Book.* London: Routledge.

Hönig, Hans G. and Paul Kussmaul (1982) *Strategie der Übersetzung. Ein Lehr- und Arbeitsbuch.* Tubingen: Narr.

House, Juliane (1997) *Translation Quality Assessment: A Model Revisited*. Tübingen: Narr.

Hung, Eva (ed.) (2002) *Teaching Translation and Interpreting 4. Building Bridges*. Amsterdam: John Benjamins.

Hurtado Albir, Amparo (1995) 'La didáctica de la traducción. Evolución y estado actual'. In José María Bravo Gozalo and Purifiación Fernández Nistal (coords.) *Perspectivas de la traducción inglés/español*. Valladolid: ICE, Universidad de Valladolid. 49-74.

------ (1996) 'La enseñanza de la traducción directa "general". Objetivos de aprendizaje y metodología'. In Amparo Hurtado Albir (ed.) *La enseñanza de la traducción*. Castellón: Universitat Jaume I. 31-56.

------ (dir.) (1999) *Enseñar a traducir. Metodología en la formación de traductores e intérpretes*. Madrid: Edelsa.

Intercultural Studies Group, Universitat Rovira i Virgili (2000) *Innovation in Translator and Interpreter Training (ITIT). An on-line symposium 17-25 January 2000*. [position papers and summaries of discussion at http://www.fut.es/~apym/symp/intro.html or in number 1 of the journal *Across Languages and Cultures*].

Jääskeläinen, Riitta (1998) 'Think-aloud Protocols'. In Mona Baker (ed.) *Routledge Encyclopedia of Translation Studies*. London: Routledge. 265-269.

Katan, David (2004) *Translating Cultures. An Introduction for Translators, Interpreters and Mediators*. Manchester: St Jerome. [2nd edition]

Kelly, David (1998) *Effective Speaking*. Huddersfield: Falcon

Kelly, Dorothy (2002) 'La competencia traductora: bases para el diseño curricular'. *Puentes* Nº 1. 9-20.

------ (2003) 'La investigación sobre formación de traductores: algunas reflexiones y propuestas'. In Emilio Ortega Arjonilla (dir.) *Panorama actual de la investigación en Traducción e Interpretación*. Granada: Atrio, vol I . 585-596

------ (2005) 'El profesor universitario de Traducción e Interpretación ante el reto del Espacio Europeo de Enseñanza Superior'. *Trans* 9, 61-72.

------ (forthcoming) 'Translator Competence Contextualized. Translator training in the framework of higher education reform: in search of alignment in curricular design'. In Dorothy Kenny and Kyongjoo Ryou (eds.) *Selected Papers from the Inaugural Conference of the International Association for Translation and Intercultural Studies, Seoul 12-14 August 2004*.

Kenny, Dorothy (1999) 'CAT Tools in an Academic Environment: What are they good for?' *Target*, 11, 1, 65-82.

Kingscott, Geoffrey (2000) 'Future Developments in International Translation'. In Wolfram Wilss (ed.) *Weltgesellschaft, Weltverkehrssprache, Weltkultur. Globalisierung versus Fragmentierung*. Tübingen: Stauffenburg. 225-234.

Kiraly, Donald (1995) *Pathways to Translation. Pedagogy and Process*. Kent, Ohio: Kent State University Press.

------ (2000) *A Social Constructivist Approach to Translator Education. Empowerment from Theory to Practice*. Manchester: St Jerome.

Klaudy, Kinga (1995) 'Quality Assessment in School vs Professional Translation'. In Cay Dollerup and Vibeke Appel (eds.) *Teaching Translation and Interpret-*

ing 3. New Horizons. Amsterdam: John Benjamins. 197-206.

Koustas, Jane (dir.) (1992) *La pédagogie de la traduction: questions actuelles. TTR,* Vol. V N°. 1.

Kussmaul, Paul (1995) *Training the Translator.* Amsterdam: John Benjamins.

Languages National Training Organization (LNTO) (2001) *The National Standards in Translating.* London: LNTO.

Li, Defeng (2000) 'Needs Assessment in Translation Teaching: Making Translator Training More Responsive to Social Needs'. *Babel,* 46:4. 289-299.

Maier, Carol (ed.) (2000) *Evaluation and Translation.* Special issue of *The Translator.* Vol. 6 N°.2.

Malmkjaer, Kirsten (ed.) (1998) *Translation and Language Teaching.* Manchester: St. Jerome.

Marchese, Theodore 'The New Conversations about Learning. Insights from Neurosciences and Anthropology, Cognitive Science and Workplace Situations'. Available from http://www.newhorizons.org/lifelong/higerh_ed/marchese.htm.

Marco, Josep (2003) 'La formación de traductores, en la encrucijada entre lo social, lo cognitivo y lo textual'. In Emilio Ortega Arjonilla (dir.) *Panorama actual de la investigación en Traducción e Interpretación.* Granada: Atrio, vol I. 597-612.

------ (2004) '¿Tareas o proyectos? ¿Senderos que se bifurcan en el desarrollo de la competencia traductora?' *Trans* N°. 8: 75-88.

Marton, Ference (1975) 'On Verbatim Training – 1: Level of processing and level of outcome'. *Scandinavian Journal of Psychology* 16. 273-279.

Martin, Ference and Roger Säljö (1984) 'Approaches to Learning'. In Ference Marton et al (eds.) *The Experiences of Learning.* Edinburgh: Scottish Academic Press.

Mayoral Asensio, Roberto (2001a) *Aspectos Epistemológicos de la Traducción.* Castellón: Universitat Jaume I.

------ (2001b) 'Por una renovación en la formación de traductores e intérpretes: revisión de algunos de los conceptos sobre los que se basa el actual sistema, su estructura y contenidos'. *Sendebar* n° 12. 311-336.

------ (forthcoming) 'La formación de traductores en el contexto universitario: crítica de la situación actual y algunas propuestas'. In Evelyne LePoder and Dorothy Kelly (eds.) *Hacia la renovación de la formación de traductores. Colección AVANTI 2.* Granada: Universidad de Granada.

Mayoral, Roberto and Dorothy Kelly (1997) 'Implications of Multilingualism in the European Union: Translator training in Spain'. In Marian B. Labrum (ed.) *The Changing Scene in World Languages. Issues and Challenges.* (ATA Scholarly Monograph Series IX) Amsterdam: John Benjamins, 19-34.

McAlester, Gerard (2000) 'The Time Factor: a practical evaluation criterion'. In Meta Grosman et al. (eds.) *Translation into Non-Mother Tongues – In Professional Practice and Training.* Tübingen: Stauffenburg. 133-140.

McCarthy, Patsy and Caroline Hatcher (2002) *Presentation Skills. The Essential Guide for Students.* London. Sage.

Neubert, Albrecht (2000) 'Competence in Language, in Languages, and in Translation'. In Christina Schäffner and Beverly Adab (eds.) *Developing Translation Competence,* Amsterdam: John Benjamins. 3-18.

Newmark, Peter (1988) *A Textbook of Translation*. London: Prentice Hall.

Newstead, Stephen E., A. Franklyn-Stokes and P. Armstead (1996) 'Individual Differences in Student Cheating'. *Journal of Educational Psychology* 88: 229-241.

Newstead, Stephen E. and Sherria Hoskins (2003) 'Encouraging Student Motivation'. In Heather Fry, Steve Ketteridge and Stephanie Marshall (eds.) (2003) *A Handbook for Teaching and Learning in Higher Education. Enhancing Academic Practice*. London: RoutledgeFalmer. 62-74.

Nord, Christiane (1991) *Text Analysis in Translation. Theory, Methodology, and Didactic Application of a Model for Translation-Oriented Text Analysis*. Amsterdam: Rodopi. [English translation of German original (1988) *Textanalyse und Übersetzen*. Heidelberg: Groos]

------ (1996a) 'El error en traducción: categorías y evaluación'. In Hurtado Albir, Amparo (ed.) *La enseñanza de la traducción*. Castellón: Universitat Jaume I. 91-108.

------ (1996b) 'Wer nimmt mal den ersten Satz? Überlegungen zu neuen Arbeitsformen im Überseztungsunterricht'. In Angelika Lauer, Heidrun Gerzymisch-Arbogast, Johann Haller and Erich Steiner (eds.) *Überseztungswissenshaft im Umbruch*. Tübingen: Narr. 313-328.

Nunan, David (1989) *Designing Tasks for the Communicative Classroom*. Cambridge: Cambridge University Press.

PACTE (2000) 'Acquiring Translation Competence: "hypotheses and methodological problems of a research project"'. In Allison Beeby et al. (eds.) *Investigating Translation*. Amsterdam: John Benjamins. 99-106.

Pym, Anthony (1992) 'Translation Error Analysis and the Interface with Language Teaching'. In Cay Dollerup and Anne Loddegaard (eds.) *Teaching Translation and Interpreting. Training, Talent, and Experience,* Amsterdam: John Benjamins, 279-290.

------ (1993) *Epistemological Problems in Translation and its Teaching*. Calaceite: Caminade.

------ (2000) *Negotiating the Frontier*. Manchester: St Jerome.

------ (2003) 'Redefining Translation Competence in an Electronic Age. In Defence of a Minimalist Approach'. *Meta* XLVIII, 4, 481-497.

------, Carmina Fallada, José Ramón Biau and Jill Orenstein (eds.) (2003) *Innovation and E-Learning in Translator Training*. Tarragona: Universitat Rovira i Virgili.

Reiss, Katharina (1976) *Texttyp und Übersetzungsmethode. Der Operative Text*. Kronberg: Scriptor.

Roberts, Roda (1984) 'Compétence du nouveau diplômé en traduction'. In *Traduction et Qualité de Langue. Actes du Colloque Société des traducteurs du Québec/ Conseil de la langue française,* Québec: Éditeur officiel du Québec. 172-184.

Robinson, Douglas (1997) *Becoming a Translator. An accelerated course*. London: Routledge. [2nd edition 2003: *Becoming a Translator. An Introduction to the Theory and Practice of Translation*]

Sager, Juan (1989) 'Quality and Standards – the evaluation of translations'. In Catriona Picken (ed.) *The Translator's Handbook*. 2nd ed. London: Aslib. 91-102.

Sánchez, Dolores (1997) 'La traducción especializada: un enfoque didáctico para los textos científicos (español-francés)'. In Miguel Ángel Vega Cernuda and

Rafael Martín Gaitero (eds.) *La palabra vertida. Investigaciones en torno a la traducción.* Madrid: Universidad Complutense de Madrid, 1997. 457-462.

------ (2004) 'Documentación y competencia traductora en la clase de traducción de textos científicos'. In Emilio Ortega Arjonilla (dir.) *Panorama actual de la investigación en Traducción e Interpretación.* Granada: Atrio, 349-356.

Schaeffner, Christina and Beverly Adab (eds.) (2000) *Developing Translation Competence.* Amsterdam: John Benjamins.

Shreve, Gregory (2000) 'Translation at the Millennium: prospects for the evolution of a profession'. In Peter Schmitt (ed.) *Paradigmenwechsel in der Translation. Festschrift für Albrecht Neubert zum 70. geburtstag.* Tübingen: Stauffenburg. 217-234.

Teichler, Ulrich and Wolfgang Steube (1991) 'The Logics of Study abroad Programmes and their Impacts'. *Higher Education.* Vol. 21 N°.3. 325-349.

Teichler, Ulrich and Volfer Jahr (2001) 'Mobility during the Course of Study and after Graduation'. *European Journal of Education.* Vol. 36. N° 4. 443-458.

Tight, Malcolm (ed.) (2003) *The RoutledgeFalmer Reader in Higher Education.* London: RoutledgeFalmer.

Tsokaktsidou, Dimitra (2005) *Los estudiantes de intercambio en el aula: una guía de buenas prácticas.* Granada: Universidad de Granada.

Vienne, Jean (1994) 'Towards a Pedagogy of "Translation in Situation"'. *Perspectives* 2 (1): 51-59.

Villa, Manuel (2004) 'Educadores orientados al aprendizaje'. In Francisco Michavila y Jorge Martínez (eds.) *La profesión de profesor de universidad.* Madrid: Cátedra UNESCO de Gestión y Política Universitaria. 53-60.

Waddington, Christopher (1999) *Estudio comparativo de diferentes métodos de evaluación de traducción general (inglés-español).* Doctoral thesis. Madrid: Universidad Pontificia Comillas.

Wakeford, Richard (2003) 'Principles of Student Assessment'. In Heather Fry, Steve Ketteridge and Stephanie Marshall (eds.) *A Handbook for Teaching and Learning in Higher Education. Enhancing Academic Practice.* London: RoutledgeFalmer. 42-61.

Way, Catherine (2000) 'Structuring Specialised Translation Courses: A hit and Miss Affair?'. In Christina Schaeffner and Beverly Adab (eds.) *Developing Translation Competence.* Vol. 38 Benjamins Tanslation Library. Amsterdam/ Philadelphia: John Benjamins. 131-141.

------ (2002) 'Traducción y Derecho: iniciativas para desarrollar la colaboración interdisciplinar'. *Puentes* 2: 15-26.

------ (forthcoming) 'El talón de Aquiles: un modelo para la autoevaluación formativa'. In Evelyne LePoder and Dorothy Kelly (eds.) *Hacia la renovación de la formación de traductores. Colección AVANTI 2.* Granada: Universidad de Granada.

Wilss, Wolfram (1976) 'Perspectives and Limitations of a Didactic Framework for the Teaching of Translation'. In Richard W. Brislin (ed.) *Translation Applications and Research,* New York: Gardner. 117-137.

Wisdom, James and Graham Gibbs (1994) *Course Design for Resource Based Learn-*

ing. Humanities. Oxford: Oxford Centre for Staff Development.

Working Group Basic Skills, Entrepreneurship and Foreign Languages (2003) *Implementation of 'Education and Training 2010' Work Programme: Progress Report.* Unpublished working document. European Commission, Directorate-General for Education and Culture.

Websites consulted or referred to

Academic Cooperation Association: http://www.aca-secretariat.be

American Translators Association: www.atanet.org

Aquarius website for professional translators: http://www.aquarius.net

Bundesverband der Dolmetscher und Übersetzer: http://www.bdue.de

CIUTI: www.ciuti.org

Colegio de Traductores Públicos de la Ciudad de Buenos Aires: http://www.traductores.org.ar

Consortium for Training Translation Teachers: http://isg.urv.es/cttt/cttt/cttt.html

European Association for Quality Assurance in Higher Education: http://www.enqa.net

European Commission (translator profile): http://europa.eu.int/comm/dgs/translation/workingwithus/recruitment/translator_profile_en.htm

European Society for Translation Studies (EST): http://www.est-translationstudies.org

Institute for Translation and Interpreting: http://www.iti.org.uk

Intercultural Studies Group. Translator Training Observatory: http://isg.urv.es/tti/tti.htm

International Association for Translation and Intercultural Studies (IATIS): http://www.iatis.org

International Federation of Translators (FIT): http://www.fit-ift.org

International Network for Quality Assurance Agencies in Higher Education: http://www.inqaahe.org

Irish Translators' and Interpreters' Association: http://www.translatorsassociation.ie

Korean Society of Translators: http://www.kstinc.co.kr

Localization Industry Standards Association (LISA): http://www.lisa.org

National Centre for Languages, CILT: http://www.cilt.org.uk

New Zealand Society of Translators and Interpreters: http://www.nzsti.org

ProZ website for professional translators: http://www.proz.com

Société Française des Traducteurs: http://www.sft.fr

South African Translators' Institute: http://www.translators.org.za

Support4learning (resources for advisors, students and everyone involved in education, training and communities): http://support4learning.org.uk/careers/work_exp.htm

Temcu Socrates Action 6 Project on training teaching staff for the multicultural classroom arising from mobility programmes: http://www.temcu.com

Tradutech: http://www.tradutech.net

Tuning Project: http://www.relint.deusto.es/TuningProject/index.htm

Universitat de Vic trainer training seminar: http://www.uvic.es/fchtd/especial/en/collaborative_translation_teaching.html

Index